PYTHON

PROGRAMMING
FOR BEGINNERS

Will Boxer

TABLE OF CONTENTS

PART I
LAYING THE FOUNDATION

CHAPTER 1
PYTHON UNLEASHED

UNDERSTANDING PYTHON'S POWER AND POPULARITY

In the vast ecosystem of programming languages, Python shines bright as one of the most popular and powerful tools at a developer's disposal. Its rise to prominence is no accident but the result of a unique blend of simplicity, versatility, and a robust community of enthusiasts and professionals alike. As an aspiring tech entrepreneur, diving into Python's realms presents an exciting avenue to bring your tech ideas to life. The allure of Python isn't merely a result of its coding elegance but a testament to how it has been embraced by industries far and wide.

Python's narrative began in the late 1980s, conceived by Guido van Rossum as a successor to the ABC language. It was aimed to address the gaps in ease of code readability and accessibility that other languages lacked at the time. Over the decades, it has morphed into a force majeure in the programming world, a tool of choice for many programmers, data scientists, and tech innovators.

One of the hallmarks of Python is its simplicity. The language prides itself on its readability and ease of learning. With a syntax that emphasizes clarity and reduces the complexities often found in other programming languages, Python is a welcoming entry point for newcomers to the coding world. It is this simplicity that can propel you from concept to code to creation with ease, a trajectory that's essential for tech entrepreneurs keen on transforming ideas into viable products swiftly.

Yet, the simplicity doesn't detract from Python's capabilities. It's a language robust enough to tackle complex problems. Its vast array of libraries and frameworks extend its functionality, making it a suitable tool for various tasks ranging from web development, data analysis, artificial intelligence, machine learning, and more. Whether you're looking to analyze large datasets to make informed business decisions, or developing a web application for your startup, Python's extensive ecosystem is up for the challenge.

Let's talk about the community. The Python community is a cornerstone of its popularity. It's a vibrant, supportive, and ever-growing community that embodies a culture of sharing and collaboration. This community has contributed a plethora of libraries and frameworks which enhance Python's utility and application. Additionally, the collective wisdom and the willingness of experienced Pythonistas to mentor and support newcomers is a remarkable asset. As you embark on your Python learning journey, you're not alone; you are backed by a community eager to see you succeed.

Python's popularity isn't confined to a niche but spreads across various sectors. It's the language of choice in academia for scientific computing, a favored tool among data scientists for statistical analysis, and a trusted ally for web developers. The commercial sector, too, has embraced Python; tech giants like Google, Facebook, and Spotify, to name a few, have harnessed Python's power to solve real-world problems and fuel innovation.

The popularity and power of Python come with a promise - a promise of opening doors to technological advancements and providing a solid foundation for those with the zeal to solve real-world problems. It's not just a programming language; it's a tool with the potential to shape ideas into realities, making it a quintessential skill for aspiring tech entrepreneurs.

Moreover, the ease with which Python can be learned and applied means that you do not need to be a seasoned programmer to start building. With a plethora of resources available, both online and offline, learning Python has never been easier. As you flip through the pages of this book, each chapter will unveil the layers of Python, gradually building your understanding and skill, preparing you for the journey of transforming your tech ideas into tangible solutions.

In the subsequent chapters, we will delve deeper into setting up your Python environment, writing your first Python program, and navigating through the essential elements of Python programming. Each step is designed to bring you closer to mastering Python, thus enabling you to exploit its potentials towards achieving your entrepreneurial aspirations in the tech world.

As we embark on this journey together, remember, every line of code you write is a step closer to turning your ideas into reality. With Python as your ally, the world of tech entrepreneurship is within your grasp.

INSTALLING AND SETTING UP PYTHON ENVIRONMENT

Embarking on the journey of Python programming begins with setting up the Python environment on your machine. This initial step is akin to laying the foundation stone of a building. A smooth installation process and a well-set environment are crucial for a hassle-free learning experience. This section will guide you through a step-by-step process to install Python and set up the necessary environment, ensuring a solid ground to kickstart your Python programming journey.

Python is known for its ease of installation and configuration, which is a boon especially for those who are transitioning from a non-technical background. Let's break down the installation and setup process into simple, manageable steps.

Step 1: Downloading Python

The first step is to download the Python installer. Visit the official Python website at https://www.python.org/downloads. Here, you'll find the option to download Python. It's advisable to download the latest version to ensure you have access to the latest features and security updates.

```
Note: Ensure you have a stable internet connection to download the installer without
interruptions.
```

Step 2: Running the Installer

Once the installer is downloaded, locate the file on your computer, typically found in the Downloads folder. Double-click on the installer to initiate the installation process. You'll be presented with a window that has a checkbox at the bottom that says "Add Python X.Y to PATH" (where X.Y is the version number). It's essential to check this box as it allows the easy execution of Python from the command line.

```
Tip: Adding Python to PATH is a crucial step that aids in running Python from the
Command Prompt or Terminal with ease.
```

Click on the `Install Now` option to proceed. The installer will now take care of the installation process, and within a few minutes, Python should be installed on your machine.

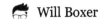

Step 3: Verifying the Installation

Post-installation, it's good practice to verify the installation to ensure everything is set up correctly. Open your command prompt or terminal (depending on your operating system), and type the following command:

```
python --version
```

This command should return the version of Python that you installed, confirming that Python was installed successfully.

Step 4: Setting Up the Integrated Development Environment (IDE)

An Integrated Development Environment (IDE) is a software application that provides a conducive environment for programming. While Python does come with its IDE called IDLE, there are other robust IDEs like PyCharm or Visual Studio Code that offer a plethora of features designed to aid in writing, testing, and debugging code efficiently.

Download and install an IDE of your choice. Post installation, launch the IDE, and familiarize yourself with the interface. Explore the menus and settings, and ensure you are comfortable navigating around.

```
Note: An IDE is not mandatory, but it significantly enhances the coding experience
by providing a structured environment, especially for large projects.
```

Step 5: Running Your First Python Script

Now that you have Python and an IDE installed, it's time to write and run your first Python script. Open your IDE, create a new file, and type the following code:

```
print("Hello, World!")
```

Save the file with a `.py` extension, for instance, `hello.py`. Now run the script. You should see `Hello, Python!` displayed in the output.

These steps lay the groundwork for your Python programming journey. Ensuring a smooth installation and setup process is pivotal as it eliminates potential roadblocks, allowing you to focus on learning and experimenting with Python. The simplicity of setting up Python is one of the many attributes that make Python a preferred choice among new and experienced developers alike.

Transitioning from a corporate role to a tech entrepreneur role involves wearing many hats, and one of those is becoming proficient in Python to bring your ideas to life. A well-set Python environment is your first stride towards mastering Python, building your tech products, and eventually, launching your tech startup. This guide aims to provide a seamless setup experience, laying a robust foundation for the subsequent chapters, where we will delve deeper into the core concepts of Python programming.

As you proceed, remember, the essence of Python lies in its simplicity and efficiency, and setting it up is just the beginning. With every new line of code, you unravel a world filled with endless possibilities, steering closer to your entrepreneurial aspirations in the tech domain.

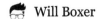

YOUR FIRST PYTHON PROGRAM

Having installed Python and set up the environment, it's time to dive into the exciting world of programming by creating your first Python program. This moment is like the first step on fresh snow, the beginning of a journey filled with discovery and empowerment. Remember, every tech entrepreneur started with a single line of code, just like you're about to.

Writing Your First Script

Let's begin with something simple yet gratifying. We'll create a script that outputs "Hello, World!" — a traditional first program for many programmers.

Open your Integrated Development Environment (IDE) and create a new file. Now, type the following line of code:

```
print("Hello, World!")
```

Save this file as `hello.py`. The `.py` extension signifies that it's a Python file. Now, run this file within your IDE or through the command line using the following command:

```
python hello.py
```

You should see `Hello, World!` displayed on the screen. Congratulations! You've just written and executed your first Python program. Though simple, this program is the starting point of endless possibilities.

Understanding the Code

Now, let's dissect this program to understand what we just did.

The `print()` function is a built-in Python function that outputs text to the console. Whatever text you place between the parentheses, enclosed in quotes, is what will be displayed.

Expanding Your Program

Now, let's expand this program by adding a couple more `print()` statements:

```
print("Hello, World!")
print("Welcome to the exciting journey of Python programming.")
print("Let's build something amazing!")
```

When you run this program, each sentence will appear on a new line in the console. This is because the `print()` function adds a newline character at the end by default.

Comments: Your Program's Annotation

In programming, it's essential to document your code to explain what certain parts of the code are doing. These explanations are for you, or other programmers who might work with your code in the future. In Python, you write comments by starting the line with a hash (`#`) symbol.

```
# This is a comment
print("Hello, World!")   # This is also a comment
```

Comments are ignored by the Python interpreter and don't affect how your program runs. However, they are crucial for understanding the code, especially as programs become more complex.

Errors: They are Your Friends

Don't be afraid of errors. They are your friends, seriously! Errors provide feedback and help you understand what went wrong. For example, if you forget to close the quotes around the text and run the program, you'll see an error like this:

```
SyntaxError: EOL while scanning string literal
```

This error is telling you that Python reached the "End Of Line" (EOL) while looking for the closing quote. Errors lead you towards the right path, correcting your code.

Practice Makes Perfect

The mantra of mastering programming is practice. Try modifying the program, change the text, add more `print()` statements, introduce new errors deliberately to understand the error messages, and fix them.

Reflection

Reflecting on what you've learned is a crucial step in the learning process. You've learned how to create a simple program, understood the importance of comments, and seen how errors can guide you.

As you transition from a corporate role to tech entrepreneurship, every line of code you write sharpens your problem-solving skills, fuels your creativity, and takes you one step closer to your tech entrepreneurial goals. This simple program is your gateway to building complex, real-world applications that solve problems and add value to your target audience.

The journey from writing `Hello, World!` to developing a Minimum Viable Product (MVP) for your startup is filled with learning, excitement, and growth. Embrace the process, learn from every line of code, and remember, every big achievement begins with the decision to try.

Now, as you progress through this book, you'll build upon this basic knowledge, explore more complex concepts, and work on real-world projects that align with your entrepreneurial aspirations in the tech domain. So, gear up, as the world of Python programming unfolds, promising a journey filled with learning, creativity, and endless opportunities to make a significant impact in the tech world.

EXERCISES

Exercise 1.3.1

- **Task:** Write a Python program to display your name and age.

Exercise 1.3.2

- **Task:** Modify the program to display the number of days you have lived.

CHAPTER 2
NAVIGATING PYTHON

BASIC SYNTAX AND STRUCTURE

As you transition into the realm of Python, understanding its basic syntax and structure is crucial. Python is known for its simplicity and readability, enabling you to craft clean, efficient, and easily understandable code. This chapter aims to introduce you to the fundamental syntax and structural elements of Python that will serve as the building blocks for your programming journey.

The Beauty of Simplicity

Python's syntax is designed to be intuitive and its readability fosters a collaborative coding environment. This simplicity is not a limitation but a feature, which helps in maintaining a clean codebase and reducing the cognitive load on you as a developer, especially when you are juggling between your corporate responsibilities and your tech entrepreneurial aspirations.

Indentation: The Cornerstone of Python's Structure

Unlike many programming languages that use braces `{}` to denote blocks of code, Python uses indentation. This is a significant aspect of Python's syntax and ensures that the code is neat and readable.

```
if 5 > 2:
    print("Five is greater than two!")
```

In this example, the `print` statement is indented to indicate that it belongs to the `if` block. The indentation must be consistent throughout your program; otherwise, Python will raise an error.

Comments: Your Coding Diary

Comments are essential for explaining your code, and are marked by a `#` symbol. They are ignored by Python's interpreter, allowing you to write notes or explain your logic.

```
# This is a comment explaining the following code
print("Hello, World!")
```

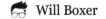

Variables: Naming Your Data

Variables are used to store data values. Python has no command for declaring a variable; you create a variable at the moment you first assign a value to it.

```
x = 5
y = "John"
```

In this example, `x` is a variable storing the integer value `5`, and `y` is a variable storing the string value `"John"`.

Data Types: Knowing Your Data

Python supports numerous data types like integers, float (decimal numbers), string (text), and boolean (True/False). Knowing the type of data you are working with is essential, and Python provides the `type()` function to ascertain a variable's data type.

```
x = 5
print(type(x))    # Output: <class 'int'>
```

Operators: Manipulating Data

Operators are symbols used to perform operations on variables and values. Python includes a variety of operators, such as addition `+`, subtraction `-`, multiplication `*`, and division `/`.

```
x = 5
y = 3
print(x + y)    # Output: 8
```

Control Flow: Directing Your Program

Control flow tools, like conditional statements and loops, allow your program to execute different code blocks depending on certain conditions.

```
if x > y:
    print("x is greater than y")
elif x < y:
    print("x is less than y")
else:
    print("x and y are equal")
```

Functions: Modular Blocks of Code

Functions are blocks of code designed to do one specific job, which can be called with a name. Functions help in organizing code, making it more readable and reusable.

```python
def greet():
    print("Hello, World!")

greet()  # Output: Hello, World!
```

Importing Modules: Extending Functionality

Python's functionality can be extended with the use of modules. Modules are files containing a set of functions you can include in your application.

```python
import math
print(math.sqrt(16))  # Output: 4.0
```

Practice: The Path to Mastery

To consolidate your understanding of Python's basic syntax and structure, indulge in writing code snippets. Create variables, manipulate them with operators, make decisions with control flow tools, define functions, and explore modules.

Embracing the Journey

As you delve into Python's syntax and structure, remember that every line of code you write is a step closer to realizing your tech entrepreneurial dreams. The simplicity of Python is your ally, enabling you to focus on solving real-world problems and building your startup's MVP. Each concept introduced in this chapter lays the foundation for more complex topics, preparing you for the exciting challenges ahead. With the basics now in your toolkit, you're ready to explore deeper waters, enrich your understanding, and move closer to becoming a proficient Python programmer capable of bringing your tech entrepreneurial visions to life.

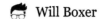
EXERCISES

Exercise 2.1.1

- **Task:** Write a Python program to calculate the sum of three given numbers.

Exercise 2.1.2

- **Task:** Write a Python program to swap the values of two variables.

VARIABLES AND DATA TYPES EXPLORATION

Embarking on the expedition of Python, the first companions you encounter are variables and data types. They form the bedrock upon which the edifice of your programming knowledge will rise. This sub-chapter unfurls the world of variables and data types in Python, aiding you in forming a strong grasp that will be instrumental in your tech-entrepreneurial journey.

Variables: The Stalwarts of Storage

Variables are like containers in the digital world, holding data that can be manipulated throughout a program. They can store a myriad of data types, and the data within can be replaced or altered as needed.

```python
# Defining a variable
message = "Hello, Python!"
print(message)  # Output: Hello, Python!
```

In Python, a variable is created the moment you first assign a value to it, and it can be re-assigned with a new value anytime, which can also be of a different data type.

```python
message = 123  # Now, the variable holds an integer value
print(message)  # Output: 123
```

Data Types: The Essence of Variables

Every variable in Python has a data type, which dictates the type of value it can hold. Here's a closer glance at some fundamental data types:

Integer:

Integers are whole numbers without a decimal point.

```python
age = 25
```

Float:

Floating-point numbers possess a decimal point.

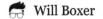

```
price = 19.99
```

String:

Strings are sequences of characters enclosed within single, double, or triple quotes.

```
greeting = 'Hello, World!'
```

Boolean:

Booleans represent one of two values: True or False.

```
is_active = True
```

Python also supports complex numbers, lists, tuples, dictionaries, and sets among other data types which will be delved into in later chapters.

Type Conversion: Morphing Data Types

At times, you may need to convert data from one type to another, which can be done using type conversion functions like `int()`, `float()`, `str()`, etc.

```
initial_price = "19.99"
final_price = float(initial_price)
```

Dynamic Typing: A Glimpse of Flexibility

Python is dynamically typed, which means that the type of data a variable holds can be changed during runtime.

```
value = 45  # integer
value = "Hello"  # Now it's a string
```

Immutable vs Mutable Types: A Key Distinction

Immutable types like integers, floats, strings, and tuples cannot be changed after they are created. On the flip side, mutable types like lists, dictionaries, and sets can be altered.

```python
# Immutable
name = "Alice"
# Mutable
friends_list = ["Bob", "Charlie"]
friends_list.append("Dave")
```

Variable Naming Conventions: The Road to Readable Code

Adhering to naming conventions is pivotal for writing clear and maintainable code. Variable names should be descriptive, using lowercase letters and underscores to separate words.

```python
# Good practice
user_age = 25

# Not recommended
UserAge = 25   # This follows the CamelCase convention, which is not preferred in
Python for variable names
```

Practice Makes Perfect: Embarking on Exercises

The path to mastering variables and data types is laden with practical exercises. Try creating various variables, explore different data types, and manipulate them. Here are some exercises to ignite your journey:

1. Create a variable to store your age and another to store your favorite quote.

2. Convert a floating-point number to an integer and observe the change.

3. Experiment with type conversion, especially between strings, integers, and floats.

The Voyage Ahead

As you delve deeper into the realm of variables and data types, remember, each stride takes you closer to the realm of tech entrepreneurship. The understanding of variables and data types is fundamental, as they will recurrently appear, playing a crucial role in the programs you'll craft to bring your startup ideas to fruition. With a solid grasp of these foundational concepts, you're well on your way to unlocking the potential of Python and propelling your tech entrepreneurial dreams into reality. Your quest for Python mastery is well underway, with each line of code weaving the fabric of your tech entrepreneurial dreams.

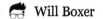

EXERCISES

Exercise 2.2.1

- **Task:** Write a Python program to check the data type of a variable.

Exercise 2.2.2

- **Task:** Write a Python program to convert an integer to a float.

OPERATORS AND EXPRESSIONS

As you venture into the realms of Python, you'll soon encounter operators, the tools that allow you to perform operations on variables and values. Expressions, on the other hand, are combinations of values and operators that can be evaluated to produce a result. This sub-chapter aims to equip you with a solid understanding of operators and expressions, which are pivotal in writing effective Python programs for your entrepreneurial endeavors.

Understanding Operators

Operators are the building blocks of Python programs. They are used to perform operations such as addition, subtraction, multiplication, and division. Let's delve into the various types of operators available in Python:

Arithmetic Operators:

These operators are used for arithmetic calculations.

```python
# Example:
a = 10
b = 20

addition = a + b   # Output: 30
subtraction = a - b   # Output: -10
multiplication = a * b   # Output: 200
division = a / b   # Output: 0.5
```

Comparison Operators:

These operators are used to compare values.

```python
# Example:
a = 10
b = 20

is_equal = (a == b)   # Output: False
is_not_equal = (a != b)   # Output: True
```

Logical Operators:

Logical operators are used to combine conditional statements.

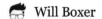

```
# Example:
a = True
b = False

and_operation = a and b   # Output: False
or_operation = a or b   # Output: True
```

Assignment Operators:

These operators are used to assign values to variables.

```
# Example:
a = 10
a += 20   # Equivalent to a = a + 20; Now a is 30
```

Identity and Membership Operators:

Identity operators (`is`, `is not`) check if two variables are located on the same part of the memory, while membership operators (`in`, `not in`) test whether a value or variable is found in a sequence.

```
# Example:
list_1 = [1, 2, 3, 4]
2 in list_1   # Output: True
```

Expressions: The Symphony of Operators and Values

Expressions are combinations of values, variables, operators, and calls to functions. When you type an expression on the command line, Python evaluates it and displays the result.

```
# Example:
expression_result = 10 + 20 * 30 / 10   # Output: 70.0
```

Evaluating Expressions: The Order of Operations

Understanding the order in which operations are performed is crucial for correctly evaluating expressions. Python follows the standard order of operations as used in mathematics.

```
# Example:
result = (10 + 20) * 30 / 10   # Output: 90.0; parentheses alter the order of
operations
```

The Power of Expressions: Simplifying Complex Calculations

Expressions empower you to perform complex calculations with ease. By combining various operators, you can create expressions that simplify complex calculations, making your code more readable and maintainable.

```
# Example:
total_cost = (20 + 30) * 10 / 5   # This expression computes the total cost based on
some formula
```

Exercises: Sharpening Your Operator and Expression Skills

1. Create expressions using each of the operator types discussed above.

2. Evaluate complex expressions, altering the order of operations using parentheses.

3. Experiment with identity and membership operators with different data types.

Reflections: The Significance of Operators and Expressions

Mastering operators and expressions is a stepping stone towards writing efficient and effective Python code. As you venture into developing your tech startup, these concepts will be instrumental in creating algorithms that drive your business logic. Moreover, understanding how to manipulate and evaluate expressions will streamline your problem-solving process, propelling you closer to your entrepreneurial goals.

Your venture into the heart of Python continues to unveil the vast potential that lies in mastering this robust programming language. As you traverse through the layers of operators and expressions, you're not only learning to communicate with the machine but also laying down the framework of logic that will drive your tech startup to success. The journey continues to be exhilarating, with each operator and expression you encounter, opening new vistas of possibilities. With every line of code, you're not just writing a program, but you're scripting the narrative of your entrepreneurial saga.

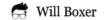 Will Boxer

EXERCISES

Exercise 2.3.1

- **Task:** Write a Python program to calculate the area of a rectangle.

Exercise 2.3.2

- **Task:** Write a Python program to calculate the perimeter of a circle.

.

CHAPTER 3
DECISION MAKING AND LOOPS

CONDITIONAL STATEMENTS

In the realm of programming, decision-making is a crucial facet that enables the logical flow of execution. Just as in life, where our actions are often dictated by certain conditions, in Python too, you can dictate the flow of your program using conditional statements. As an aspiring tech entrepreneur, mastering this concept will be instrumental in building intelligent, responsive software applications.

The Essence of Conditional Statements

Conditional statements in Python are your gateway to creating decisions in your code. They evaluate whether a certain condition is true or false, and then execute a specific block of code accordingly. Let's explore the different types of conditional statements available in Python.

The if Statement:

The `if` statement is the most straightforward form of conditional logic. It evaluates a condition and executes a block of code only if the condition is true.

```
# Example:
age = 28
if age > 18:
    print("You are eligible to vote.")
```

In this example, since the condition `age > 18` is true, the message "You are eligible to vote." will be printed.

The elif Statement:

`elif`, a contraction of 'else if', checks another condition if the previous condition(s) were false.

```
# Example:
age = 16
if age >= 18:
    print("You are eligible to vote.")
elif age < 18:
    print("You are too young to vote.")
```

Here, since `age >= 18` is false, Python evaluates the next condition `age < 18`, which is true, thus printing "You are too young to vote."

The else Statement:

The `else` statement catches anything which isn't caught by the preceding conditions.

```
# Example:
age = 18
if age > 18:
    print("You are eligible to vote.")
else:
    print("You are just old enough to vote.")
```

In this case, since `age > 18` is false, the `else` statement is executed, printing "You are just old enough to vote."

Nesting and Compound Conditions

You can nest `if` statements within each other for more complex logic, and use logical operators (`and`, `or`, `not`) to create compound conditions.

```
# Example:
age = 25
citizenship = 'USA'
if age >= 18:
    if citizenship == 'USA':
        print("You are eligible to vote in the USA.")
    else:
        print("You are not eligible to vote in the USA.")
```

Practical Scenarios: Where Conditional Statements Shine

Imagine you're building a simple application for your startup that requires age verification for sign-up. Utilizing `if`, `elif`, and `else` statements will be essential in creating the logic that verifies a user's age.

```
# Example:
user_age = 17   # Assume this value is input by the user
if user_age >= 18:
    print("Sign-up successful.")
else:
    print("Sorry, you must be at least 18 years old to sign up.")
```

Reflecting on the Power of Conditional Statements

Conditional statements are the crux of logical decision-making in your Python programs. They empower your code to react differently to different inputs, making your applications dynamic and responsive. As you tread the path of tech entrepreneurship, you'll find conditional statements to be indispensable in building applications that solve real-world problems. Whether it's verifying user inputs, directing program flow, or making real-time decisions, conditional statements are a cornerstone of effective programming.

In your endeavor to transition from a corporate role to a tech entrepreneur, mastering conditional statements is a significant stride towards building a solid foundation in Python. As you forge ahead, the ability to make informed decisions in code will translate into making astute decisions in your entrepreneurial journey, steering your startup towards success in the tech arena.

With every `if`, `elif`, and `else`, you're not just crafting conditions in code, but you're laying down the conditions for your success in the tech-driven entrepreneurial world. So, embrace the logical prowess of conditional statements, and take a decisive step towards realizing your tech entrepreneurial aspirations.

EXERCISES

Exercise 3.1.1

- **Task:** Write a Python program to check if a number is positive, negative, or zero.

Exercise 3.1.2

- **Task:** Write a Python program to check if a number is odd or even.

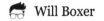 Will Boxer

LOOPING STRUCTURES

Just as rivers have currents that flow ceaselessly, driven by the pull of gravity, programs too have a flow, directed by the logic embedded within them. In Python, looping structures let you iterate through tasks, enabling your code to execute commands repeatedly under specified conditions. These loops are the currents of your program, channeling the flow of execution.

Unveiling the Power of Loops

Looping structures in Python are a boon to programmers, facilitating the execution of a block of code multiple times. This is a timesaver and a code optimizer, allowing you to accomplish repetitive tasks with minimal code. Let's dive into the different types of loops Python has to offer.

The For Loop:

A `for` loop in Python is utilized to iterate over a sequence or other iterable objects. Iterating over sequences is done till the last item is reached.

```python
# Example:
for number in range(1, 6):
    print(number)   # This will print numbers 1 through 5
```

In this simple example, `number` takes on the values in the range 1 to 5, printing each one.

The While Loop:

A `while` loop continues execution as long as a specified condition is met. It's like saying, "while this is true, do that."

```python
# Example:
counter = 0
while counter < 5:
    print(counter)   # This will print numbers 0 through 4
    counter += 1
```

Here, as long as `counter` is less than 5, the code within the loop will execute, printing the current value of `counter`.

Control Flow in Loops

You can control the flow of your loops using break and continue statements, which will be discussed in detail in the next sub-chapter. However, here's a brief introduction:

- `break`: Exits the loop prematurely when a certain condition is met.

- `continue`: Skips the rest of the current loop iteration and proceeds to the next iteration.

Nesting Loops:

Python allows for loops to be nested within each other, creating a loop of loops, each with its own scope.

```python
# Example:
for outer in range(3):
    for inner in range(3):
        print(outer, inner)
```

This nested loop will iterate over both ranges, printing pairs of numbers from 0 to 2.

Practical Applications of Looping Structures:

The real power of loops shines through in practical applications. For instance, if you're building an app for your startup, you might need to process a list of user data. Loops can automate repetitive tasks, such as data validation or generation of user profiles.

```python
# Example:
user_data = [{'name': 'Alice', 'age': 30}, {'name': 'Bob', 'age': 25}, {'name':
'Charlie', 'age': 35}]
for user in user_data:
    print(f"Name: {user['name']}, Age: {user['age']}")
```

In this snippet, a `for` loop iterates through a list of user data dictionaries, printing out the name and age of each user.

Reflecting on the Looping Paradigm:

Looping structures are among the pillars that hold the logic edifice of your program. They breathe life into your code, enabling it to dance to the rhythm of logic, iterating through tasks and processing data efficiently. As you immerse yourself in the art of coding, you'll find loops to be your loyal companions, tirelessly executing tasks, reducing the redundancy in your code, and bringing your applications closer to the realm of real-world problems that they aim to solve.

As you endeavor to transition into the tech-entrepreneurial space, mastering loops will empower you to write efficient, clean, and optimized code. It's akin to having an adept orchestra conductor leading a harmonious rendition of complex musical pieces, where each loop is a musician playing the notes of logic in a rhythmic ensemble.

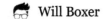 Will Boxer

With every iteration, with every loop, you're not just running code; you're iterating through the possibilities, looping through the challenges, and inching closer to the harmonious melody of success. So harness the power of loops, iterate through the learning curve, and keep looping in the melody of Python's logic until your tech-entrepreneurial dreams manifest into reality.

EXERCISES

Exercise 3.2.1

- **Task:** Write a Python program to print numbers 1 to 10 using a for loop.

Exercise 3.2.2

- **Task:** Write a Python program to find the sum of all numbers from 1 to n.

BREAK, CONTINUE, AND PASS STATEMENTS

In the realm of programming, control over the flow of execution is paramount. It's the rhythm to which every line of code dances. In this sub-chapter, we delve into three choreographers of this rhythm in Python - the `break`, `continue`, and `pass` statements. These are the tools that help finesse the flow of loops, rendering control and precision to the choreography of code execution within loops.

Break Statement

In the dance of programming, a `break` statement is your cue for an abrupt exit. It terminates the loop and transfers the execution to the next statement following the loop.

```
for i in range(10):
    if i == 5:
        break
    print(i)
```

In this code snippet, the loop will cease its iteration when `i` equals 5. The numbers 0 through 4 will be printed, but not any further.

Continue Statement

The `continue` statement is akin to a graceful leap over a beat, skipping the rest of the loop's body for the current iteration, leaping straight into the next.

```
for i in range(10):
    if i % 2 == 0:
        continue
    print(i)
```

Here, the `continue` statement causes the loop to skip the print statement for even numbers. Only the odd numbers between 0 and 9 get printed.

Pass Statement

The `pass` statement is the quiet observer in the room. It does nothing when executed, acting as a placeholder.

```
for i in range(10):
    if i % 2 == 0:
        pass   # This will do nothing and the loop will continue
    print(i)
```

In this snippet, every number between 0 and 9 gets printed, despite the `pass` statement. It's a placeholder, biding its time for future code.

Employing Control Statements in Real-World Scenarios

Let's envision a real-world scenario, fitting for our aspiring tech entrepreneurs. Suppose you are processing a list of transactions for your start-up. Your goal is to identify and process only the transactions above a certain value, while disregarding the smaller transactions.

```
transactions = [150, 200, 950, 75, 300, 700]
for transaction in transactions:
    if transaction < 200:
        continue
    # Process transaction
    print(f'Processed transaction of value: {transaction}')
```

In this scenario, the `continue` statement helps to skip the processing of transactions below 200, thus optimizing the process by only allocating resources to significant transactions.

Reflecting on Control Flow

The `break`, `continue`, and `pass` statements are more than mere keywords. They are the maestros of control flow, each with its unique style of conducting the code. The `break` statement is the decisive conductor, bringing a segment to an abrupt close when required. The `continue` statement is the agile dancer, gracefully skipping over beats yet keeping the rhythm intact. The `pass` statement is the silent choreographer, awaiting its script, yet keeping the stage ready.

As you march forward on the path of tech entrepreneurship, these control flow statements are your allies. They help you script the narrative of your code, ensuring it aligns with the logic envisioned in your mind. They are the unsung heroes that work behind the scenes, ensuring your code performs in a controlled, predictable manner, no matter the complexity of the logic it encapsulates.

In the next chapter, we will venture into the heart of functions and modules, continuing our journey towards mastering Python. But for now, take a moment to reflect on the control flow statements, practice them, and envision how they can serve your entrepreneurial aspirations. They are simple, yet powerful, shaping the flow of logic in your code, ensuring it dances to the rhythm of your entrepreneurial dreams.

EXERCISES

Exercise 3.3.1

- **Task:** Write a Python program to find the first multiple of 7 in a range of numbers from 1 to 50.

Exercise 3.3.2

- **Task:** Write a Python program to skip printing numbers 4 and 7 in a range of numbers from 1 to 10.

PART II
DIVING DEEPER

CHAPTER 4
FUNCTIONS AND MODULES

DEFINING FUNCTIONS

The heartbeats of Python's flexibility are functions. They encapsulate logic into reusable blocks, promoting code reusability, organization, and clarity. As an aspiring tech entrepreneur transitioning from a corporate role, mastering functions is your step towards building robust and modular code for your startup ventures.

The Anatomy of a Function

A function is defined using the `def` keyword, followed by the function name, a pair of parentheses, and a colon. The function body follows, indented consistently. Let's break down a basic function:

```python
def greet(name):
    """This function greets the person passed in as a parameter"""
    print(f"Hello, {name}!")
```

Here, `greet` is the function name, and `name` is the parameter. The string in triple quotes is a docstring, explaining what the function does.

Calling a Function

To summon the behavior encapsulated in a function, you `'call'` it by its name followed by parentheses. Parameters required by the function are placed within these parentheses.

```python
greet('Alice')
```

This call will output: `Hello, Alice!`.

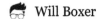

Parameters and Arguments

Parameters are the names used when defining a function, whereas arguments are the values passed to the function when it's called. Parameters are the function's inputs. Our `greet` function has one parameter: `name`. When we called `greet('Alice')`, the argument `'Alice'` was passed to `greet`.

Default Parameter Values

You can specify default values for parameters. If an argument for such a parameter is omitted when the function is called, the default value is used.

```python
def greet(name='World'):
    print(f"Hello, {name}!")

greet()   # Outputs: Hello, World!
```

Return Values

Functions can also return values. This is done using the `return` statement, followed by the value to return.

```python
def add(a, b):
    return a + b

sum_result = add(5, 3)   # sum_result is now 8
```

Variable Scope

Variables defined within a function have a local scope, making them inaccessible outside the function. However, variables defined outside all functions have a global scope, accessible anywhere within the program.

```python
x = 10   # Global variable

def display_number():
    x = 5   # Local variable
    print(x)   # Outputs: 5

display_number()
print(x)   # Outputs: 10
```

Practical Application: Creating a Basic Calculator

Let's now encapsulate some logic in a function to create a basic calculator capable of addition, subtraction, multiplication, and division.

```python
def calculate(operation, a, b):
    if operation == 'add':
        return a + b
    elif operation == 'subtract':
        return a - b
    elif operation == 'multiply':
        return a * b
    elif operation == 'divide':
        return a / b if b != 0 else "Cannot divide by zero"

# Usage:
result = calculate('add', 5, 3)
print(result)   # Outputs: 8
```

EXERCISES

Exercise 4.1.1

- **Task:** Write a Python function to calculate the factorial of a number.

Exercise 4.1.2

- **Task:** Write a Python function to check if a number is prime.

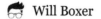

MODULES AND PACKAGES

As you delve deeper into the realm of Python, understanding the modularity it offers is indispensable. Modules and packages are the essence of reusability and organization, allowing you to structure your code logically and keep it clean. This is especially vital for aspiring tech entrepreneurs who aim to build scalable and maintainable tech solutions.

Understanding Modules

A module is a file containing Python statements and definitions. For instance, a file named `example.py` is a module named `example`. Modules allow you to organize your code, encapsulating related functions, variables, and classes into separate files, which can then be reused across other projects.

Creating a module is as straightforward as saving a `.py` file. Here's a simple module that defines a function to calculate the sum of two numbers:

```python
# Save this as calculator.py
def add(a, b):
    return a + b
```

Importing Modules

To use the functionalities defined in a module, you need to import it using the `import` statement followed by the module name:

```python
import calculator

sum_result = calculator.add(5, 3)
print(sum_result)   # Outputs: 8
```

Aliasing Modules

You can also create an alias for a module, which can be useful to shorten long module names or to standardize imports if multiple developers are working on a project.

```python
import calculator as calc

sum_result = calc.add(5, 3)
```

Exploring the Standard Library

Python comes with a vast standard library, a collection of modules providing implementations for many operations like file I/O, system calls, and even interfaces to graphical user interface toolkits like Tk.

For instance, the `math` module provides mathematical functions:

```
import math

print(math.sqrt(16))    # Outputs: 4.0
```

Understanding Packages

A package is a way of organizing related modules into a directory hierarchy. Essentially, it's a directory with a special file named `__init__.py`, which may be empty but indicates that the directory is a Python package.

Here's a simple structure of a package:

```
mypackage/
    __init__.py
    submodule1.py
    submodule2.py
```

Importing from Packages

You can import individual modules from a package, using the dot (.) operator to navigate through the package structure.

```
import mypackage.submodule1

mypackage.submodule1.some_function()
```

Practical Application: Creating a Utility Package

Let's create a utility package for a hypothetical startup. This package will have different modules for various utilities like string manipulations, mathematical calculations, and date operations.

```
startup_utilities/
    __init__.py
    string_utils.py
    math_utils.py
    date_utils.py
```

Each module will have related functions. For instance, `string_utils.py` could have functions for capitalizing all words in a string, and `math_utils.py` could have functions for basic arithmetic operations.

EXERCISES

Exercise 4.2.1

- **Task:** Create a module named `operations.py` with a function to calculate the sum of two numbers.

Exercise 4.2.2

- **Task:** Import the `math` module and use it to calculate the square root of a number.

PRACTICAL EXAMPLES OF BUILT-IN FUNCTIONS

Python, a versatile language, comes with a plethora of built-in functions to ease the journey of coders. These functions are the unsung heroes, ready to be summoned upon your command, making your code concise and readable. This sub-chapter unfolds the magic of some of these functions through practical examples. It is not just about learning the syntax, but grasping the essence of how these functions can be the catalyst in solving real-world problems, especially for our aspiring tech entrepreneurs ready to dive into the tech realm.

The `len()` Function: Measuring the Length

The `len()` function, a simple yet powerful tool, returns the number of items in an object.

```python
# Example: Length of a list
my_list = [1, 2, 3, 4, 5]
length = len(my_list)
print(length)  # Output: 5
```

The `max()` and `min()` Functions: Finding Extremes

These functions help in identifying the maximum and minimum values from a sequence or a set of values.

```python
# Example: Max and Min in a list
my_list = [34, 78, 23, 56, 89]
print(max(my_list))  # Output: 89
print(min(my_list))  # Output: 23
```

The `sorted()` Function: Organizing Data

`sorted()` function is a lifesaver when it comes to arranging data in a specific order (ascending by default).

```python
# Example: Sorting a list of numbers
my_list = [34, 78, 23, 56, 89]
sorted_list = sorted(my_list)
print(sorted_list)  # Output: [23, 34, 56, 78, 89]
```

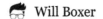

The `sum()` Function: Adding Up Values

`sum()` simplifies the task of adding up all the numbers in a sequence.

```python
# Example: Sum of a list of numbers
my_list = [34, 78, 23, 56, 89]
total = sum(my_list)
print(total)   # Output: 280
```

The `map()` Function: Transforming Data

`map()` is a boon for applying a function to every item in a sequence, returning an iterator.

```python
# Example: Square all numbers in a list
my_list = [1, 2, 3, 4, 5]
squared_list = list(map(lambda x: x*x, my_list))
print(squared_list)   # Output: [1, 4, 9, 16, 25]
```

The `filter()` Function: Sifting Through Data

`filter()` assists in extracting elements from a sequence for which a function returns True.

```python
# Example: Filter out odd numbers from a list
my_list = [1, 2, 3, 4, 5]
even_list = list(filter(lambda x: x % 2 == 0, my_list))
print(even_list)   # Output: [2, 4]
```

EXERCISES

Exercise 4.3.1

- **Task:** Write a Python program to find the maximum of three numbers using the `max` function.

Exercise 4.3.2

- **Task:** Write a Python program to round a floating-point number to 2 decimal places.

CHAPTER 5
DATA HANDLING AND MANIPULATION

WORKING WITH LISTS, TUPLES, AND DICTIONARIES

In the realm of Python, Lists, Tuples, and Dictionaries are fundamental data structures that hold the potential to store, organize, and manipulate data. As aspiring tech entrepreneurs on the verge of launching a tech startup, harnessing the power of these data structures is crucial in building robust, efficient applications. This sub-chapter unfolds the core concepts of Lists, Tuples, and Dictionaries, illustrated through practical examples that resonate with real-world scenarios.

Lists: Your Go-to Data Storehouse

Lists in Python are akin to dynamic size arrays, capable of storing heterogeneous types of data - be it integers, floats, strings, or even other lists and data structures.

```python
# Creating a list
my_list = [1, 2, 3, "hello", 5.5]

# Accessing elements
print(my_list[3])   # Output: hello
```

Adding and Removing Elements

```python
# Adding elements
my_list.append(6)   # my_list now becomes [1, 2, 3, "hello", 5.5, 6]

# Removing elements
my_list.remove("hello")   # my_list now becomes [1, 2, 3, 5.5, 6]
```

Tuples: The Immutable Lists

Tuples are similar to lists but with a prime distinction - immutability. Once created, they cannot be altered, which makes them a reliable choice for storing data that should remain unchanged throughout the program's lifetime.

```
# Creating a tuple
my_tuple = (1, 2, 3, "hello", 5.5)

# Accessing elements
print(my_tuple[3])   # Output: hello
```

Dictionaries: The Key to Quick Data Retrieval

Dictionaries are unparalleled when it comes to data retrieval. They store data in key-value pairs, enabling quick access to values based on unique keys.

```
# Creating a dictionary
my_dict = {"name": "John", "age": 30, "city": "New York"}

# Accessing values
print(my_dict["name"])   # Output: John
```

Adding and Removing Key-Value Pairs

```
# Adding key-value pairs
my_dict["country"] = "USA"   # my_dict now becomes {"name": "John", "age": 30,
"city": "New York", "country": "USA"}

# Removing key-value pairs
del my_dict["city"]   # my_dict now becomes {"name": "John", "age": 30, "country":
"USA"}
```

EXERCISES

Exercise 5.1.1

- **Task:** Write a Python program to find the length of a list.

Exercise 5.1.2

- **Task:** Write a Python program to merge two dictionaries.

FILE HANDLING TECHNIQUES

File handling is a quintessential aspect of programming that transcends across various domains, be it data analysis, web development, or artificial intelligence. At the core, file handling is about storing data in a persistent manner, so it remains intact between different runs of your program, and retrieving it back when necessary. Python furnishes a straightforward and effective way of working with files, which is a boon for aspiring tech entrepreneurs aiming to build a minimum viable product (MVP) for their startup ideas.

Opening and Closing Files

Before you can read from or write to a file, you need to open it using Python's built-in `open()` function. This function returns a file object that provides methods and attributes to perform various operations on the file.

```python
# Opening a file in read mode
file = open('example.txt', 'r')

# Closing the file
file.close()
```

Reading from Files

Once a file is opened, you can read its content using several methods such as `read()`, `readline()`, or `readlines()`.

```python
# Reading the entire file
file = open('example.txt', 'r')
content = file.read()
file.close()
print(content)

# Reading one line at a time
file = open('example.txt', 'r')
line = file.readline()
file.close()
print(line)

# Reading all lines into a list
file = open('example.txt', 'r')
lines = file.readlines()
file.close()
print(lines)
```

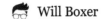

Writing to Files

Writing to files is as simple as reading from them. You can use the `write()` or `writelines()` methods to write text to files.

```python
# Writing to a file
file = open('example.txt', 'w')
file.write('Hello, World!')
file.close()

# Writing multiple lines to a file
file = open('example.txt', 'w')
lines = ['Hello, World!', 'Python is fun.']
file.writelines(lines)
file.close()
```

Working with Files in a Safe Manner

It's a good practice to work with files in a way that ensures they are closed after use, which can be achieved using the `with` statement.

```python
# Using with statement for file operations
with open('example.txt', 'r') as file:
    content = file.read()
print(content)  # File is automatically closed after exiting the block
```

EXERCISES

Exercise 5.2.1

- **Task:** Write a Python program to read the contents of a file.

Exercise 5.2.2

- **Task:** Write a Python program to write a list of strings to a file.

EXCEPTION HANDLING ESSENTIALS

Exception handling is a crucial technique for developing robust and reliable software. In Python, exceptions are events that can modify the flow of control through a program. They arise from errors occurring during the program's execution, and if unhandled, can cause the program to terminate abruptly. This sub-chapter explores the essential practices for handling exceptions in Python, ensuring your program can respond gracefully to errors, which is a critical aspect of building a resilient Minimum Viable Product (MVP) for your startup.

Understanding Exceptions

An exception in Python is an object that represents an error. When a Python script encounters a situation, it cannot cope with, it raises an exception. This could be due to various reasons such as a file not found, dividing by zero, or an incorrect input.

```python
# Example of an exception
try:
    result = 10 / 0
except ZeroDivisionError:
    print("You cannot divide by zero!")
```

The Try-Except Block

The primary mechanism for handling exceptions in Python is the try-except block. It allows you to attempt the execution of code that may raise exceptions and to handle those exceptions if they occur.

```python
try:
    # Code that may raise an exception
    result = int("Invalid Integer")
except ValueError as e:
    # Handling the exception
    print(f"An error occurred: {e}")
```

Multiple Exception Handlers

You can have multiple except blocks to handle different exceptions. This practice enables more fine-grained control and response to various error conditions.

```
try:
    # Code that may raise an exception
    file = open("non_existent_file.txt", "r")
    content = file.read()
    value = int(content)
except FileNotFoundError:
    print("The file was not found.")
except ValueError:
    print("The file content is not a valid integer.")
```

The Else and Finally Clauses

The `else` clause in a try-except block executes if no exception occurs, and the `finally` clause executes no matter what, providing a mechanism for cleanup code.

```
try:
    # Code that may not raise an exception
    print("Everything is working fine.")
except:
    print("An error occurred.")
else:
    print("No exceptions occurred.")
finally:
    print("Cleaning up, this code runs no matter what.")
```

Raising Exceptions

In some situations, you may need to generate exceptions explicitly. The `raise` statement allows you to throw exceptions programmatically, which can be caught elsewhere in your code.

```
def validate_age(age):
    if age < 0:
        raise ValueError("Age cannot be negative")

try:
    validate_age(-5)
except ValueError as e:
    print(f"Validation failed: {e}")
```

EXERCISES

Exercise 5.3.1

- **Task:** Write a Python program to handle a division by zero error.

Exercise 5.3.2

- **Task:** Write a Python program to handle multiple exceptions.

CHAPTER 6
OBJECT-ORIENTED PYTHON

CLASSES AND OBJECTS

Transitioning into the tech entrepreneurial realm demands a solid grasp of object-oriented programming (OOP) principles. This is where Python's classes and objects come into play, enabling you to model real-world entities, encapsulate data, and build scalable, maintainable software solutions for your startup ventures. This sub-chapter unfolds the essentials of defining classes and creating objects in Python, providing a stepping stone towards harnessing the power of OOP for your projects.

Understanding Classes

Classes are the blueprints for objects, encapsulating data and behavior that objects will possess. They embody a high level of abstraction, allowing you to model real-world entities in a code-friendly manner.

```python
class Car:
    def __init__(self, brand, model, year):
        self.brand = brand
        self.model = model
        self.year = year
```

In this example, `Car` is a class representing a car entity, with attributes for brand, model, and year. The `__init__` method is the constructor, initializing new instances of the `Car` class with specific data.

Instantiating Objects

Objects are instances of classes, embodying the data and behavior defined in the class blueprint.

```python
my_car = Car('Toyota', 'Corolla', 2020)
```

Here, `my_car` is an object of the `Car` class, initialized with 'Toyota' as the brand, 'Corolla' as the model, and 2020 as the year.

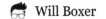 Will Boxer

Accessing Attributes and Methods

Objects house attributes and methods, which are accessed using dot notation.

```python
print(my_car.brand)    # Output: Toyota

my_car.model = 'Camry'   # Updating the model attribute
```

In this snippet, we access the `brand` attribute and update the `model` attribute of `my_car`.

Defining Methods

Methods encapsulate behavior within classes, enabling interactions with or operations on the object's data.

```python
class Car:
    # Existing code omitted for brevity

    def start_engine(self):
        print(f"The {self.model}'s engine is now running.")

my_car.start_engine()   # Output: The Camry's engine is now running.
```

The `start_engine` method, defined within the `Car` class, prints a message when called on an object.

Encapsulation

Encapsulation restricts direct access to some of the object's components, promoting a robust and maintainable codebase.

```python
class Car:
    # Existing code omitted for brevity

    def __update_mileage(self, miles):
        self.mileage += miles

    def drive(self, miles):
        self.__update_mileage(miles)
        print(f"Driving for {miles} miles.")

my_car.drive(100)
```

Here, the `__update_mileage` method is encapsulated, ensuring it's only accessible within the `Car` class, while the `drive` method is publicly accessible.

EXERCISES

Exercise 6.1.1

- Task: Write a Python class to represent a Rectangle with methods to calculate area and perimeter.

Exercise 6.1.2

- Task: Write a Python class to represent a Circle with methods to calculate area and circumference.

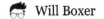 Will Boxer

INHERITANCE AND POLYMORPHISM

Inheritance and polymorphism are two pillars of Object-Oriented Programming (OOP) that propel the efficiency and manageability of your code. These concepts are quintessential for tech entrepreneurs diving into software development, enabling you to build scalable, maintainable systems that can evolve over time as your startup grows.

Inheritance: The Backbone of Reusability

Inheritance facilitates the creation of a new class based on an existing class, promoting code reusability and a hierarchical organization of classes.

```python
class Vehicle:
    def __init__(self, make, model):
        self.make = make
        self.model = model

class Car(Vehicle):
    def __init__(self, make, model, doors):
        super().__init__(make, model)
        self.doors = doors

my_car = Car('Toyota', 'Corolla', 4)
```

In this example, `car` inherits from `vehicle`. The `super()` function calls the constructor of the parent class, allowing `car` to initialize the `make` and `model` attributes defined in `vehicle`.

The Power of Overriding

Overriding empowers a subclass to provide a specific implementation for a method that is already defined by its superclass or by one of its superclasses.

```python
class Vehicle:
    def fuel_efficiency(self):
        return 'Generic fuel efficiency'

class Car(Vehicle):
    def fuel_efficiency(self):
        return 'Car-specific fuel efficiency'

my_car = Car()
print(my_car.fuel_efficiency())  # Output: Car-specific fuel efficiency
```

Here, `car` overrides the `fuel_efficiency` method of `vehicle`, providing a car-specific implementation.

Polymorphism: Flexibility in Action

Polymorphism allows methods to do different things based on the object it is acting upon, even when they share the same interface.

```python
class Truck(Vehicle):
    def fuel_efficiency(self):
        return 'Truck-specific fuel efficiency'

def display_fuel_efficiency(vehicle):
    print(vehicle.fuel_efficiency())

my_truck = Truck('Ford', 'F-150')
display_fuel_efficiency(my_car)      # Output: Car-specific fuel efficiency
display_fuel_efficiency(my_truck)    # Output: Truck-specific fuel efficiency
```

The `display_fuel_efficiency` function illustrates polymorphism. It can operate on any object that implements a `fuel_efficiency` method, regardless of the object's class.

Mixins: Enhancing Flexibility

Mixins provide a way to share methods across multiple classes, further enhancing code reusability and organization.

```python
class ElectricMixin:
    def battery_capacity(self):
        return 'Generic battery capacity'

class ElectricCar(ElectricMixin, Car):
    pass

my_electric_car = ElectricCar('Tesla', 'Model S', 4)
print(my_electric_car.battery_capacity())  # Output: Generic battery capacity
```

`ElectricCar` inherits both from `Car` and `ElectricMixin`, gaining access to the methods defined in `ElectricMixin`.

EXERCISES

Exercise 6.2.1

- **Task:** Write a Python program to demonstrate inheritance by creating a class `Square` that inherits from `Rectangle`.

Exercise 6.2.2

- **Task:** Write a Python program to demonstrate polymorphism by creating a method that takes any shape object and returns its area.

REAL-WORLD APPLICATIONS OF OOP

Object-Oriented Programming (OOP) is not merely a theoretical concept but a practical programming paradigm extensively utilized in real-world applications. Its principles are instrumental in building robust, scalable, and maintainable software. For aspiring tech entrepreneurs transitioning from corporate roles, understanding the real-world applications of OOP is pivotal. It provides a lens through which complex systems can be understood, designed, and optimized.

Software Modularity

Modularity is at the heart of OOP. It encourages the decomposition of a software system into smaller, interchangeable, and upgradeable modules. Each module, encapsulated in a class, represents a separate concern. This separation of concerns simplifies the development, testing, and maintenance of software systems.

```python
class User:
    def __init__(self, username, password):
        self.username = username
        self.password = password

class Authentication:
    def login(self, user):
        # Logic for user login

    def logout(self, user):
        # Logic for user logout
```

In this simplistic illustration, `User` and `Authentication` are separate modules with distinct responsibilities.

Design Patterns

Design patterns are solutions to common software design problems. They represent templates devised to help solve problems in a more efficient and maintainable way. OOP principles form the backbone of many design patterns, enabling the creation of advanced system architectures.

For instance, the Singleton Pattern ensures a class has only one instance and provides a global point of access to that instance.

```python
class Singleton:
    _instance = None

    def __new__(cls):
        if cls._instance is None:
            cls._instance = super().__new__(cls)
        return cls._instance

singleton1 = Singleton()
singleton2 = Singleton()
print(singleton1 == singleton2)   # Output: True
```

Frameworks and Libraries

Numerous modern frameworks and libraries adopt OOP principles. Frameworks like Django and Flask for web development, or libraries like Pandas and NumPy for data analysis, are built around OOP concepts, making it easier to extend and customize their functionalities.

Game Development

In the realm of game development, OOP is indispensable. It helps model and manage complex game systems, where each object can have properties and behaviors, making the codebase organized and extensible.

```python
class Character:
    def __init__(self, name, health):
        self.name = name
        self.health = health

    def take_damage(self, damage):
        self.health -= damage

class Enemy(Character):
    def attack(self, target):
        # Logic for enemy attack
```

Here, game entities like characters and enemies are modeled using classes and inheritance.

User Interface Development

OOP plays a pivotal role in user interface (UI) development. It helps in organizing and managing the codebase in a way that separates the logic from the presentation, facilitating the creation of dynamic and interactive UIs.

```
class Button:
    def __init__(self, label):
        self.label = label

    def on_click(self):
        # Logic for button click

class Dialog:
    def __init__(self, title):
        self.title = title
        self.buttons = []

    def add_button(self, button):
        self.buttons.append(button)
```

In this illustration, UI elements like buttons and dialogs are encapsulated in classes.

Database Management

OOP, combined with Object-Relational Mapping (ORM), simplifies database management. It allows developers to work with databases using programming objects, eliminating the need for SQL.

```
class UserModel:
    def __init__(self, username, email):
        self.username = username
        self.email = email

    def save(self):
        # Logic to save user data to database
```

The `UserModel` class represents a user in the database, and methods like `save` handle the database interactions.

EXERCISES

Exercise 6.3.1

- **Task:** Write a Python class to represent a Bank Account with methods to deposit and withdraw money.

Exercise 6.3.2

- **Task:** Write a Python class to represent a Product with methods to set and get product price, and calculate the total cost for a given quantity.

PART III
ADVANCED PYTHON TECHNIQUES

CHAPTER 7
PYTHON LIBRARIES AND FRAMEWORKS

INTRODUCTION TO NUMPY AND PANDAS

As we venture into more advanced territories of Python programming, it's essential to get acquainted with libraries that can significantly augment our capabilities, making the process of data handling, analysis, and visualization much more straightforward and efficient. Two such libraries that stand out are NumPy and Pandas, known for their vast utility in data science and analytical tasks.

NumPy: Numerical Python

NumPy, short for Numerical Python, is a library that provides support for large, multi-dimensional arrays and matrices, along with a collection of mathematical functions to operate on these data structures. The core functionality of NumPy revolves around the `ndarray` (n-dimensional array) object, providing a high-performance environment for mathematical operations on vectors and matrices.

```python
import numpy as np

# Creating a NumPy array
arr = np.array([1, 2, 3, 4, 5])

# Performing a mathematical operation on the array
arr_add = arr + 5
print(arr_add)   # Output: [6 7 8 9 10]
```

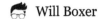

The snippet above illustrates the creation of a NumPy array and a simple operation of adding a scalar value to each element of the array.

Pandas: Data Manipulation and Analysis

On the other hand, Pandas is a high-level data manipulation tool developed on top of NumPy. It provides data structures like Series and Data Frame, alongside the essential functionality required for cleaning, aggregating, transforming, visualizing, and more.

```python
import pandas as pd

# Creating a DataFrame
data = {
    'Name': ['Alice', 'Bob', 'Charlie'],
    'Age': [25, 30, 35]
}
df = pd.DataFrame(data)

# Accessing data
print(df['Name'])   # Output: 0 Alice, 1 Bob, 2 Charlie
```

In this snippet, a Pandas Data Frame is created from a dictionary, and data is accessed using column labels.

Bridging Real-World Data

NumPy and Pandas together form a potent duo for tackling real-world data challenges. They serve as the backbone for many data science projects, providing the tools necessary for working with data at scale, be it cleaning data, performing statistical analysis, or preparing data for machine learning models.

For instance, consider a scenario where you have collected customer feedback for your startup's product. The data, filled with textual reviews and numerical ratings, is messy and unstructured. Here, Pandas could be employed to clean and structure the data, making it ready for analysis. On the other hand, NumPy could assist in performing numerical analysis, like calculating average ratings or measuring the variance in customer feedback.

```python
# Assuming df is your DataFrame containing customer feedback
average_rating = np.mean(df['Rating'])
rating_variance = np.var(df['Rating'])
```

EXERCISES

Exercise 7.1.1

- **Task:** Write a Python program to create a NumPy array of 10 zeros.

Exercise 7.1.2

- **Task:** Write a Python program to create a Pandas Series from a list.

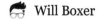

Data Visualization with Matplotlib and Seaborn

The essence of data visualization is to communicate information clearly and efficiently to users via the graphical representation of data. It's about translating complex datasets into visual formats that are intuitive and easy to understand, yet insightful. The ability to visualize data is crucial for tech entrepreneurs as it helps in identifying patterns, trends, and insights, aiding informed decision-making. Python, with its robust libraries Matplotlib and Seaborn, provides a fertile ground for data visualization.

Matplotlib: The Gateway to Data Visualization

Matplotlib is a widely used plotting library for the Python programming language. It's designed to create static, animated, and interactive visualizations in Python. The simplicity and flexibility of Matplotlib make it a go-to library for generating plots, histograms, power spectra, bar charts, error charts, scatterplots, and more.

```python
import matplotlib.pyplot as plt

# Simple line plot
x = [1, 2, 3, 4, 5]
y = [2, 3, 5, 7, 11]
plt.plot(x, y)
plt.xlabel('X-axis Label')
plt.ylabel('Y-axis Label')
plt.title('Simple Line Plot')
plt.show()
```

In the snippet above, we use Matplotlib to create a simple line plot. We first import the library, define our data, create the plot, label the axes, title the plot, and finally display it using `plt.show()`.

Seaborn: Statistical Data Visualization

Seaborn, built on top of Matplotlib, is a high-level interface for drawing attractive and informative statistical graphics. It comes with several built-in themes and color palettes to make statistical plots more attractive. Seaborn is well-suited for visualizing complex datasets with multiple variables.

```python
import seaborn as sns
import pandas as pd

# Load data
data = sns.load_dataset("tips")

# Create a boxplot
sns.boxplot(x="day", y="total_bill", data=data)
plt.show()
```

Here, we use Seaborn to create a box plot of a dataset, demonstrating the distribution of total bill amounts for different days of the week.

Insights Through Visualization

Data visualization is not merely about generating plots but about deriving actionable insights. For instance, you may want to analyze the user engagement metrics of your startup's app. By visualizing the data, you can identify peak usage times, preferences of different user segments, and areas needing improvement.

Practical Exercise: Sales Performance Analysis

Scenario: You have obtained sales data from various channels of your tech startup. The data consists of date, sales amount, channel, and region.

Task: Utilize Matplotlib to plot the sales trends over time, compare sales performance across different channels and regions. Employ Seaborn to visualize the distribution of sales amounts and identify any outliers that may exist.

```python
# Assuming df is your DataFrame containing sales data
# Matplotlib for trend analysis
plt.plot(df['date'], df['sales_amount'])
plt.title('Sales Trend Over Time')
plt.xlabel('Date')
plt.ylabel('Sales Amount')
plt.show()

# Seaborn for distribution analysis
sns.boxplot(x="channel", y="sales_amount", data=df)
plt.title('Distribution of Sales Amount by Channel')
plt.show()
```

This exercise provides a hands-on experience on how you can use Matplotlib and Seaborn to derive insights that can help in strategizing sales and marketing efforts for your startup.

Bridging Visualization to Action

Visualization is a bridge between the quantitative content and the actionable insights derived from it. Effective visualization helps in compressing the complex data into digestible chunks that can be used to make informed decisions. For tech entrepreneurs, this could mean identifying the right market segments, understanding user behavior, optimizing operational processes, or even pitching to investors with compelling data stories.

Conclusion

The journey from data to decision is a critical one. Matplotlib and Seaborn serve as reliable companions on this journey, enabling you to visualize data in a manner that is both insightful and telling. As you proceed with building your startup, these visualizations will not only guide your decisions but also serve as a powerful tool for communicating your ideas and results to stakeholders, be it your team, investors, or customers. The practical exercises included will ensure that you grasp the application of these libraries in real-world scenarios, aligning with your objective of building a strong foundation in Python for your entrepreneurial venture.

The beauty of Python lies in its vast ecosystem of libraries, which are like pieces of a puzzle. As you fit these pieces together, you form a clearer picture of the landscape ahead, enabling you to navigate the complex yet exciting world of tech entrepreneurship with confidence and foresight. Through each line of code, you are not just writing a script, but scripting the narrative of your startup's journey in the tech realm.

EXERCISES

Exercise 7.2.1

- **Task:** Write a Python program to create a line plot with Matplotlib.

Exercise 7.2.2

- **Task:** Write a Python program to create a bar plot with Seaborn.

WEB DEVELOPMENT WITH FLASK AND DJANGO

Web development is a crucial skill for tech entrepreneurs, especially those looking to create tech-based solutions or startups. Being proficient in web development not only allows you to build and iterate on your Minimum Viable Product (MVP) swiftly but also provides the ability to communicate and interact with your target audience through the web. Python, being a versatile and powerful language, offers excellent frameworks like Flask and Django for web development. This sub-chapter aims to introduce you to these frameworks, demonstrating their capabilities and how they can be harnessed in your entrepreneurial journey.

Flask: The Lightweight Warden

Flask is a micro web framework for Python. Its 'micro' label doesn't reflect its capabilities but rather its simplicity and ease of use. With Flask, you get the freedom of a lightweight framework combined with the power of Python's extensive ecosystem.

```python
from flask import Flask
app = Flask(__name__)

@app.route('/')
def hello():
    return 'Hello, World!'

if __name__ == '__main__':
    app.run()
```

In the snippet above, you see the beauty of Flask in action. With just a few lines of code, you have a basic web application up and running. This simplicity is what makes Flask a preferred choice for beginners and for projects that require a fast-to-market approach.

Django: The Robust Conductor

On the other end of the spectrum, we have Django. It's a high-level Python web framework that encourages rapid development and clean, pragmatic design. Django follows the "Don't Repeat Yourself" (DRY) principle, which promotes code reusability.

```python
# Importing necessary Django modules
from django.shortcuts import render
from django.http import HttpResponse

# Defining a simple view
def hello(request):
    return HttpResponse("Hello, World!")
```

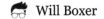 Will Boxer

The snippet illustrates a simple Django view that returns a "Hello, World!" message. While Django requires a more structured approach compared to Flask, it provides a wealth of built-in features and follows a model-template-views architectural pattern, making it a solid choice for larger applications or projects with complex requirements.

Choosing Between Flask and Django

The choice between Flask and Django largely depends on the nature and scale of your project. Flask provides more flexibility and is less opinionated, making it suitable for smaller projects or when you want more control over the components you use. Django, with its built-in features, is well-suited for larger applications where many common features are required out of the box.

Practical Exercise: Build a Simple Web Application

Scenario: You aim to create a web platform to collect feedback on your startup idea from potential customers.

Task: Build a simple web application with a form to collect user feedback. You may choose either Flask or Django for this task based on your project needs.

```python
# Using Flask
from flask import Flask, request, render_template_string

app = Flask(__name__)

@app.route('/', methods=['GET', 'POST'])
def feedback():
    if request.method == 'POST':
        feedback = request.form['feedback']
        # Process the feedback...
    return render_template_string('''<form method="post">
                                    Feedback: <input type="text"
                                    name="feedback"><br>
                                    <input type="submit" value="Submit">
                                  </form>''')

if __name__ == '__main__':
    app.run()
```

This exercise demonstrates how quickly you can get a web application running to collect user feedback, one of the critical steps in validating your startup idea.

Web Development: A Door to Interactions

Web development opens doors to user interactions, making it a vital skill in the tech entrepreneurial space. It's not just about coding but about creating value, validating ideas, and interacting with your audience. Flask and Django, each with its unique set of features, offer a pathway to develop web-based platforms efficiently.

Conclusion

Web development is more than coding; it's about building bridges between your ideas and the audience. Flask and Django are excellent companions on this journey, offering the tools and frameworks necessary to bring your web applications to life swiftly and efficiently. As you traverse the path of tech entrepreneurship, the knowledge and practical skills acquired in web development, particularly with Flask and Django, will prove to be invaluable assets. Through practical exercises and real-world scenarios, this sub-chapter aims to equip you with the foundational web development skills necessary to propel your tech entrepreneurial journey forward.

EXERCISES

Exercise 7.3.1

- **Task:** Write a simple Flask application to display "Hello, World!" on the homepage.

Exercise 7.3.2

- **Task:** Write a Django view to handle a form submission and display the submitted data.

CHAPTER 8
REAL-WORLD PYTHON APPLICATIONS

AUTOMATING TASKS

Automation is the magic wand in the realm of programming. It transforms tedious, manual tasks into swift, error-free processes with a single command. As aspiring tech entrepreneurs transitioning from corporate roles, you're about to dive into a realm where time is of the essence, and efficiency is the currency. Automating routine tasks is a crucial step towards achieving more in less time. Python, with its rich ecosystem, offers a myriad of libraries and tools for automation, making your entrepreneurial journey smoother and more efficient.

The Philosophy of Automation

Automation is not about eliminating the human element; it's about augmenting human capabilities, freeing you from mundane tasks, and giving you more time to innovate and think creatively. With Python at your disposal, you can automate various tasks such as data entry, file management, email notifications, and much more.

Your First Automated Task: File Organization

Let's start with a basic yet impactful task—organizing files on your computer. Imagine you have a folder with a mixture of files that you want to organize into sub-folders based on their file types.

```python
import os
import shutil

def organize_files(directory):
    for filename in os.listdir(directory):
        # Get the file extension and create a sub-folder
        file_ext = filename.split('.')[-1]
        sub_folder = os.path.join(directory, file_ext)
        if not os.path.exists(sub_folder):
            os.makedirs(sub_folder)
        # Move the file into the sub-folder
        shutil.move(os.path.join(directory, filename), os.path.join(sub_folder,
        filename))

# Define the directory
directory = 'path_to_your_directory'

# Call the function
organize_files(directory)
```

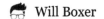

In the code snippet above, a function `organize_files` is defined, which takes a directory path as an argument. It iterates through each file in the directory, creates sub-folders based on file extensions, and moves the files into their respective sub-folders. With just a few lines of code, you've automated a task that could take hours to complete manually.

Email Automation: Keeping Stakeholders Informed

In your entrepreneurial journey, timely communication with stakeholders is crucial. Let's explore how you can automate the sending of email updates using Python.

```python
import smtplib
from email.mime.text import MIMEText

def send_email(subject, message, to_email):
    from_email = 'your_email@example.com'
    password = 'your_email_password'

    # Create the email content
    msg = MIMEText(message)
    msg['Subject'] = subject
    msg['From'] = from_email
    msg['To'] = to_email

    # Send the email
    with smtplib.SMTP_SSL('smtp.example.com', 465) as server:
        server.login(from_email, password)
        server.send_message(msg)

# Define email details
subject = 'Project Update'
message = 'The project is on track and progressing well.'
to_email = 'stakeholder@example.com'

# Send the email
send_email(subject, message, to_email)
```

In this example, the `send_email` function is created to automate the process of sending emails. This can be a game-changer in maintaining transparent communication with stakeholders, ensuring they are kept informed about project progress.

Automating Data Entry: A Step Towards Efficiency

Data entry is a task ripe for automation. Python, with libraries such as pandas, can transform data entry from a chore into a breeze.

```
import pandas as pd

def automate_data_entry(data, file_path):
    # Load existing data
    existing_data = pd.read_csv(file_path)

    # Append new data
    updated_data = existing_data.append(data, ignore_index=True)

    # Save updated data
    updated_data.to_csv(file_path, index=False)

# Define new data and file path
new_data = pd.DataFrame({'Name': ['John Doe'], 'Email': ['john.doe@example.com']})
file_path = 'path_to_your_file.csv'

# Automate data entry
automate_data_entry(new_data, file_path)
```

The `automate_data_entry` function loads existing data from a CSV file, appends new data, and saves the updated data back to the file, illustrating a simple yet powerful automation of a routine data entry task.

Conclusion

Automation is your ally in managing time and increasing productivity. By automating mundane and repetitive tasks, you not only save time but also reduce the chances of errors, enabling you to focus on the strategic aspects of your entrepreneurial venture. The examples provided in this sub-chapter serve as a stepping stone into the vast realm of automation possibilities with Python. Each automated task is a step towards a more efficient, productive, and successful entrepreneurial journey. As you explore Python's capabilities further, you'll discover a multitude of other automation opportunities that align with your venture's goals and requirements. This sub-chapter has aimed to instill a mindset of automation, encouraging you to seek opportunities where Python can take over, making your entrepreneurial path less daunting and more exhilarating.

EXERCISES

Exercise 8.1.1

- **Task:** Write a Python program to rename all files in a directory with a specific extension.

Exercise 8.1.2

- **Task:** Write a Python program to send an email using the smtplib module.

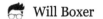

WEB SCRAPING TECHNIQUES

Web scraping is akin to a treasure hunt for data enthusiasts. It's about diving into the vast ocean of the internet and fetching pearls of data that can fuel informed decisions, especially for budding tech entrepreneurs. Web scraping is a potent tool in your arsenal, allowing you to harness data from websites and utilize it to gain insights, analyze market trends, or even scope out competition. This sub-chapter will furnish you with the techniques to effectively scrape web data using Python.

Understanding Web Scraping

Web scraping is an automated method used to extract large amounts of data from websites quickly. It's essential to note that while web scraping is a doorway to a trove of useful data, it's crucial to scrape responsibly adhering to legal and ethical guidelines.

Libraries for Web Scraping

Python boasts an array of libraries making web scraping a breeze. The two prominent libraries are Beautiful Soup and Scrapy.

- **Beautiful Soup:** A library best suited for beginners, enabling the parsing of HTML and XML documents, and effortlessly navigating through the tag soup of web pages.

```python
from bs4 import BeautifulSoup
import requests

# Fetching the webpage
response = requests.get('https://example.com')
soup = BeautifulSoup(response.content, 'html.parser')

# Extracting data
for tag in soup.find_all('a'):
    print(tag.get('href'))
```

- **Scrapy:** A more robust and feature-rich framework, empowering you to build spider bots to crawl and extract data from multiple web pages simultaneously.

```python
import scrapy

class ExampleSpider(scrapy.Spider):
    name = 'example'
    start_urls = ['https://example.com']

    def parse(self, response):
        for link in response.css('a::attr(href)').getall():
            yield {'link': link}
```

Responsibly Scraping Websites

Responsible web scraping entails adhering to the rules set by websites and ensuring your scraping activities do not adversely impact the website. Here are some guidelines:

- Robots.txt: Check the robots.txt file of a website to understand the scraping rules.

- Rate Limiting: Implement delays between requests to prevent overloading the server.

- User-Agent String: Provide a user-agent string to identify your bot.

```python
headers = {
    'User-Agent': 'YourBot/0.1 (your-email@example.com)'
}
response = requests.get('https://example.com', headers=headers)
```

Handling Dynamic Content

Many modern websites load content dynamically using JavaScript. Libraries such as Selenium can be utilized to handle such dynamic content.

```python
from selenium import webdriver

driver = webdriver.Chrome()
driver.get('https://example.com')

# Interacting with the page
element = driver.find_element_by_id('some-id')
element.click()

# Fetching dynamic content
dynamic_content = driver.page_source
driver.quit()
```

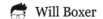

Storing Scraped Data

Once you have the desired data, it's imperative to store it in a structured format like CSV, JSON, or a database.

```python
import pandas as pd

# Assuming data is a list of dictionaries
data = [{'name': 'Alice', 'email': 'alice@example.com'}, {'name': 'Bob', 'email':
'bob@example.com'}]

# Converting to DataFrame and saving as CSV
df = pd.DataFrame(data)
df.to_csv('contacts.csv', index=False)
```

Conclusion

Web scraping is a powerful technique to fuel data-driven decisions in your entrepreneurial journey. The skills acquired here will not only help in gathering valuable data but also in understanding the market trends, thereby giving a competitive edge to your startup. This sub-chapter aimed at equipping you with the basic knowledge and techniques of web scraping, paving the way for more advanced data gathering and analysis techniques as you progress in your Python programming journey. With responsible scraping, the web turns into an open book, ready to offer its knowledge to fuel your entrepreneurial aspirations.

EXERCISES

Exercise 8.2.1

- **Task:** Write a Python program to scrape the title of a webpage using BeautifulSoup.

Exercise 8.2.2

- **Task:** Write a Python program to extract all links from a webpage using BeautifulSoup.

DEVELOPING SIMPLE WEB APPLICATIONS

Embarking on the journey of developing a web application can be exhilarating yet intimidating, especially when transitioning from a non-technical role. However, the essence of this transition lies in the real-world application of your acquired Python skills. This sub-chapter aims to gently usher you into the realm of web development, focusing on creating simple yet functional web applications.

Selecting a Web Framework

Python offers a bouquet of web frameworks, each with its unique strengths. However, for the ease of understanding and implementation, we will focus on Flask – a micro web framework that is both lightweight and powerful.

```python
from flask import Flask

app = Flask(__name__)

@app.route('/')
def home():
    return 'Hello, World!'

if __name__ == '__main__':
    app.run()
```

In the snippet above, a basic Flask application is created, which responds with "Hello, World!" when accessed.

Understanding HTTP Methods

A foundational understanding of HTTP methods is crucial as they define the type of action a web application is to perform. The primary HTTP methods include GET (retrieve data), POST (submit data), PUT (update data), and DELETE (remove data).

```python
@app.route('/form', methods=['GET', 'POST'])
def form():
    if request.method == 'POST':
        name = request.form['name']
        return f'Hello, {name}!'
    return render_template('form.html')
```

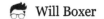

Templates and Static Files

Leveraging HTML templates and CSS files are essential to create visually appealing web applications.

```
# HTML Template: templates/home.html
<!DOCTYPE html>
<html>
<head>
    <title>Home Page</title>
</head>
<body>
    <h1>{{ message }}</h1>
</body>
</html>

# Python Script
@app.route('/home')
def home():
    message = 'Welcome to the Home Page'
    return render_template('home.html', message=message)
```

Managing Databases

Data is the lifeblood of web applications. Python, coupled with Flask, allows easy integration with databases like SQLite to manage data efficiently.

```
import sqlite3

# Connecting to the database
conn = sqlite3.connect('database.db')

# Creating a table
conn.execute('CREATE TABLE users (name TEXT, email TEXT)')
conn.close()
```

User Interaction

Creating interactive forms and handling user input are quintessential for an engaging user experience.

```
# HTML Template: templates/form.html
<form method="post">
    <label for="name">Name:</label><br>
    <input type="text" id="name" name="name" required><br>
    <input type="submit" value="Submit">
</form>

# Python Script
@app.route('/form', methods=['GET', 'POST'])
def form():
    if request.method == 'POST':
        name = request.form['name']
        return f'Hello, {name}!'
    return render_template('form.html')
```

Deploying Your Application

Once your application is ready, deploying it to a server is the next step. Heroku is a popular choice due to its simplicity and free tier offering.

```
# Procfile
web: gunicorn app:app

# requirements.txt
Flask==2.0.1
gunicorn==20.1.0

# Deploying to Heroku
$ heroku create
$ git push heroku master
```

Conclusion

The pathway of developing a simple web application encapsulates selecting a suitable framework, understanding HTTP methods, managing databases, and deploying your application. This sub-chapter has provided a glimpse into these aspects, paving the way for deeper exploration and more complex projects as you continue your Python journey. Your newly acquired skills are now a bridge, connecting your aspirations to the real tech entrepreneurial world. Each line of code you write is a step closer to transforming your startup ideas into tangible applications, propelling you further into the exhilarating realm of tech entrepreneurship. Through consistent practice and engagement with real-world projects, the once daunting world of web development will morph into a playground of endless possibilities.

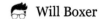 Will Boxer

EXERCISES

Exercise 8.3.1

- **Task:** Write a Python program to create a simple web application that displays a form to collect user name and age, and displays the submitted data.

Exercise 8.3.2

- **Task:** Write a Python program to create a simple REST API using Flask that returns a list of users.

CHAPTER 9
TESTING AND DEBUGGING

WRITING EFFECTIVE TESTS

Testing is an integral part of the software development cycle. As you embark on your tech entrepreneurial journey, ensuring the correctness and reliability of your code is paramount. This sub-chapter is a venture into the realm of testing in Python, aiming to equip you with the skills to write effective tests for your applications.

The Importance of Testing

In the tech entrepreneurial space, a minor bug can translate to significant losses or unsatisfied customers. Testing is your safety net, catching errors before they reach your users. It verifies that your code behaves as expected and helps in maintaining a healthy codebase as your project grows.

Choosing a Testing Framework

Python boasts several testing frameworks like `unittest`, `pytest`, and `doctest`. For our venture, we'll employ `unittest`, which comes bundled with Python and provides a solid foundation for learning testing concepts.

```python
import unittest

class TestStringMethods(unittest.TestCase):

    def test_upper(self):
        self.assertEqual('foo'.upper(), 'FOO')

if __name__ == '__main__':
    unittest.main()
```

In the above snippet, we defined a simple test case using the `unittest` framework to check the behavior of the `str.upper()` method.

Anatomy of a Test

Understanding the structure of a test is crucial. A typical test contains three phases:

1. Setup: Preparing the necessary conditions for your test.

2. Execution: Running the code you want to test.

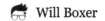

3. Assertion: Checking the result against the expected outcome.

```python
class TestMathOperations(unittest.TestCase):

    def test_addition(self):
        result = 1 + 1
        self.assertEqual(result, 2)
```

Testing Exceptions

Testing for exceptions ensures your code fails gracefully under adverse conditions.

```python
class TestException(unittest.TestCase):

    def test_divide_by_zero(self):
        with self.assertRaises(ZeroDivisionError):
            1 / 0
```

Automated Testing

Automation is the linchpin of efficient testing, allowing for the execution of a battery of tests with a single command.

```python
if __name__ == '__main__':
    unittest.main()
```

Testing Best Practices

- **Write Clear, Descriptive Test Names:** Your test names should act as documentation, indicating what behavior is being tested.

- **Keep Tests Short and Focused:** Each test should verify a single behavior.

- **Run All Tests After Each Change:** This practice helps catch regressions promptly.

- **Mock External Systems:** In testing, dependencies on external systems should be replaced with mock objects.

Putting It All Together

Now, with a rudimentary understanding of testing in Python, you're one step closer to building robust applications. The journey from a corporate role to a tech entrepreneur requires a solid grasp of testing principles to ensure your software meets the requisite standards of quality and reliability.

By embracing testing, you not only mitigate the risks associated with software bugs but also foster a culture of quality within your budding entrepreneurial venture. As you delve deeper into the Python ecosystem, the practice of writing effective tests will become second nature, bolstering your confidence and proficiency in your entrepreneurial journey.

Testing is not just a technical skill but a mindset. As you transition from understanding Python to applying it in real-world scenarios, integrating testing into your development process is a leap towards professional maturity. Each test you write is a statement of intent, an articulation of the behavior you expect from your code, and a safety net that allows you to explore, innovate, and refactor with assurance.

As you forge ahead, remember, a well-tested application is a reliable application, a critical asset in the competitive tech entrepreneurial landscape.

In the subsequent sections, we'll delve into debugging techniques, an equally vital aspect of your development journey, ensuring not just the correctness but the optimal performance of your code. Your venture into testing is the foundation upon which you build a culture of excellence, propelling you closer to your aspiration of launching a tech startup.

EXERCISES

Exercise 9.1.1

- **Task:** Write a Python program to create a unit test for a function that adds two numbers.

Exercise 9.1.2

- **Task:** Write a Python program to create a unit test for a function that raises an exception.

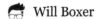

DEBUGGING TECHNIQUES

Embarking on the path of tech entrepreneurship, the ability to troubleshoot and debug your code is as essential as writing the code itself. Debugging is the process of identifying and rectifying errors within your code, ensuring that your application runs seamlessly. In this sub-chapter, we shall delve into various debugging techniques that will empower you to tackle bugs effectively, thereby bringing your MVP (Minimum Viable Product) closer to fruition.

Understanding the Bug

The first step in debugging is understanding the bug. Look for error messages, unexpected behavior, or incorrect output. The more accurately you can describe the problem, the easier it will be to solve.

```python
def divide(a, b):
    return a / b

result = divide(4, 0)  # This will raise a ZeroDivisionError
```

Print-based Debugging

The simplest form of debugging is using the `print` function to display values at different points in your code.

```python
def divide(a, b):
    print(f"Dividing {a} by {b}")
    return a / b

result = divide(4, 2)  # Output: Dividing 4 by 2
```

The Interactive Debugger (pdb)

Python provides an interactive debugger called `pdb`, which allows you to step through your code, evaluate expressions, and inspect data.

```python
import pdb

def divide(a, b):
    pdb.set_trace()
    return a / b

result = divide(4, 2)
```

Exception Handling

Utilizing exception handling not only aids in managing runtime errors but also in debugging by providing contextual information about where and why an error occurred.

```python
def divide(a, b):
    try:
        result = a / b
    except ZeroDivisionError as e:
        print(f"Error: {e}")
        return None
    return result

result = divide(4, 0)  # Output: Error: division by zero
```

Logging

Implementing logging within your code can provide a trail of events leading up to an error, which can be invaluable for debugging purposes.

```python
import logging

logging.basicConfig(level=logging.DEBUG)

def divide(a, b):
    logging.debug(f"Dividing {a} by {b}")
    return a / b

result = divide(4, 2)
```

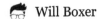

Utilizing a Profiler

A profiler helps you understand where your code spends most of its time, which can be helpful in identifying performance bugs.

```python
import cProfile

def slow_function():
    total = 0
    for i in range(1000000):
        total += i
    return total

cProfile.run('slow_function()')
```

Unit Tests

Writing unit tests can help catch bugs in your code. Tests provide a way to assert that your code behaves as expected under a variety of conditions.

```python
import unittest

class TestMathOperations(unittest.TestCase):
    def test_addition(self):
        self.assertEqual(1 + 1, 2)

if __name__ == '__main__':
    unittest.main()
```

Utilizing Code Linters and Formatters

Code linters and formatters can catch syntax errors, potential bugs, and enforce a consistent coding style, which can aid in minimizing bugs.

```python
# Using a linter like flake8 can catch potential errors
# Install flake8 via pip and run it on your file

# $ pip install flake8
# $ flake8 your_file.py
```

Continuous Integration (CI)

Implementing Continuous Integration practices, where your code is built and tested automatically, can help catch bugs early in the development process.

Debugging in a Collaborative Environment

In a collaborative setting, code reviews and pair programming are excellent ways to catch bugs. A fresh pair of eyes can often spot issues that you might have overlooked.

Developing a Debugging Mindset

Debugging can initially seem daunting, especially when transitioning from a non-technical role. However, with a structured approach and the right tools, debugging becomes an empowering process. Each bug you resolve enhances your understanding of the code and brings your entrepreneurial vision closer to reality.

Debugging is an art that requires a blend of intuition, knowledge, and a systematic approach. The techniques discussed in this sub-chapter are your toolkit to transform bugs from frustrating obstacles into opportunities for learning and improvement.

As you advance on your Python journey, the debugging skills you cultivate now will be instrumental in ensuring the robustness and reliability of your tech startup's MVP. Remember, every bug resolved is a step forward in your entrepreneurial venture, bringing you closer to launching a reliable tech product in the competitive market.

In the next sub-chapter, we will explore best practices for code maintenance, a crucial aspect that ensures the longevity and scalability of your software as your startup grows.

EXERCISES

Exercise 9.2.1

- **Task:** Write a Python program to demonstrate the use of the `pdb` module for debugging.

Exercise 9.2.2

- **Task:** Write a Python program to demonstrate the use of logging for debugging purposes.

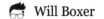 Will Boxer

BEST PRACTICES FOR CODE MAINTENANCE

The allure of launching a tech startup propels many aspiring entrepreneurs onto the path of coding. Your venture's backbone is the code that drives your Minimum Viable Product (MVP). However, the journey from code to a reliable product is often paved with maintenance endeavors. Code maintenance is the disciplined practice of keeping your codebase clean, updated, and bug-free over time, ensuring that your software remains robust and adaptable to evolving needs.

Consistent Code Style

Adhering to a consistent code style is fundamental. It promotes readability and a unified codebase, which is easier to maintain. In Python, PEP 8 is the accepted style guide. Utilize tools like `flake8` for enforcing style guidelines.

```python
# PEP 8 compliant code
def function_with_args(arg1, arg2):
    if arg1 and arg2:
        print("PEP 8 Style")

# Install flake8 and run it to check your code
# $ pip install flake8
# $ flake8 your_file.py
```

Code Comments and Documentation

Well-documented code is a gift to your future self and other developers who may work on your project. Comments should explain the *why* not the *how* of your code. Also, adhere to docstring conventions to document your functions, classes, and modules.

```python
def complex_function(x, y):
    """
    This function performs a complex operation.
    Args:
    x (int): The first parameter.
    y (int): The second parameter.

    Returns:
    int: The result of the operation.
    """
    # Some complex code here
    pass
```

Version Control

Employ version control systems like Git to track changes, collaborate with others, and revert to previous code versions when necessary.

```
# Initializing a new Git repository
$ git init
```

Code Reviews

Code reviews are an invaluable practice. They provide a second set of eyes to catch bugs, ensure consistent coding practices, and promote knowledge sharing among the team.

Refactoring

Refactoring is the art of improving code structure without altering its functionality. It's a continual process aimed at reducing technical debt and making your code more efficient, readable, and maintainable.

```python
# Before refactoring
def calculate_area(x, y):
    return x * y  # Assuming a rectangle

# After refactoring
def calculate_rectangle_area(width, height):
    return width * height
```

Automated Testing

Automated testing is your safety net. It ensures that your code behaves as expected and prevents bugs from creeping into your codebase over time.

```python
import unittest

class TestMathOperations(unittest.TestCase):
    def test_addition(self):
        self.assertEqual(1 + 1, 2)

if __name__ == '__main__':
    unittest.main()
```

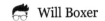

Dependency Management

Manage your project's dependencies meticulously to avoid version conflicts and ensure reproducibility. Utilize virtual environments and document your dependencies in a `requirements.txt` file.

```
# Creating a virtual environment
$ python -m venv env
# Activating the virtual environment
$ source env/bin/activate  # On Windows, use `env\Scripts\activate`
# Freezing dependencies
$ pip freeze > requirements.txt
```

Continuous Integration (CI) and Continuous Deployment (CD)

Implement CI/CD pipelines to automate testing and deployment, ensuring that your code is always in a deployable state.

Performance Monitoring

Employ monitoring tools to keep tabs on your application's performance over time, helping to spot potential issues before they escalate.

Learning from Failures

Embrace failures as learning opportunities. Analyzing bugs and understanding how they slipped through can provide invaluable insights.

Staying Updated

The tech field is ever-evolving. Keeping abreast of the latest best practices, tools, and technologies is crucial for maintaining a modern, efficient codebase.

Foster a Maintenance Mindset

Cultivating a maintenance mindset is about foreseeing the long-term implications of your coding decisions. It's about writing code that not only works today but is poised to meet the demands of tomorrow.

As an aspiring tech entrepreneur, understanding and implementing code maintenance best practices is paramount. It not only augments the longevity and reliability of your MVP but also sets a solid foundation for your startup's growth. Remember, a well-maintained codebase is a significant asset that will serve you well as you navigate the exhilarating, yet demanding, journey of tech entrepreneurship.

In the subsequent chapter, we will pivot towards leveraging Python in the professional realm, elucidating how Python intersects with various industries, and preparing you for Python job interviews. The knowledge acquired here will be instrumental as you transition from a corporate role to a tech-savvy entrepreneur, ready to make a tangible impact in the digital world.

EXERCISES

Exercise 9.3.1

- **Task:** Write a Python program to demonstrate the use of docstrings for code documentation.

Exercise 9.3.2

- **Task:** Write a Python program to demonstrate the use of a linter (e.g., flake8) to check for code style issues.

PART IV
CAREER ADVANCEMENT
WITH PYTHON

CHAPTER 10
PYTHON IN THE PROFESSIONAL WORLD

PYTHON IN DIFFERENT INDUSTRIES

As the curtain of corporate life gradually draws to a close, the exciting realm of tech entrepreneurship beckons. With Python as your loyal companion, you are about to traverse diverse industries, each with its unique set of challenges and opportunities. The versatility of Python has made it a darling across a multitude of professional domains. Let's delve into the various industries where your Python skills can be harnessed to foster innovation and drive the growth of your startup venture.

Finance

In the bustling world of finance, Python's powerful libraries like Pandas and NumPy are employed for data analysis, risk management, and algorithmic trading. The simplicity and clarity of Python code also make it an ideal choice for developing sophisticated financial models.

```
import pandas as pd
# Loading financial data for analysis
financial_data = pd.read_csv('financial_data.csv')
```

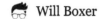

Healthcare

Healthcare is another sector where Python is making significant inroads. It's used in predictive analytics to forecast patient admissions, manage resources efficiently, and in the development of health informatics solutions.

```python
import sklearn
# Predictive modeling in healthcare
```

E-commerce

The e-commerce realm thrives on data. Python, with its vast array of data handling libraries, helps in customer segmentation, recommendation systems, and sales forecasting which are crucial for enhancing user experience and boosting sales.

```python
from sklearn.cluster import KMeans
# Customer segmentation
```

Manufacturing

Python finds utility in manufacturing for process optimization, predictive maintenance, and supply chain management, ensuring smooth operations and cost efficiency.

```python
import tensorflow as tf
# Predictive maintenance
```

Education

In education, Python is used to develop adaptive learning platforms, automate administrative tasks, and analyze educational data to improve learning outcomes.

```python
import django
# Developing an adaptive learning platform
```

Entertainment

The entertainment industry leverages Python for content recommendation, customer engagement analytics, and streamlining digital asset management, creating captivating experiences for audiences.

```
import pytorch
# Content recommendation system
```

Real Estate

Python assists in market analysis, property valuation, and predictive modeling in the real estate sector, aiding in informed decision-making.

```
import matplotlib.pyplot as plt
# Market analysis visualization
```

Environmental Science

Environmental scientists employ Python to model climate change, analyze ecological data, and in the development of conservation strategies.

```
import seaborn as sns
# Climate change modeling visualization
```

Your quest towards tech entrepreneurship will likely intersect with one or more of these industries. The beauty of Python lies in its adaptability and the vast community that continually enriches its ecosystem with cutting-edge libraries and frameworks. This makes Python a formidable tool regardless of the industry you choose to venture into.

As you transition from the structured corporate environment to the dynamic tech entrepreneurial space, Python's versatility will prove to be an invaluable asset. The practical examples and exercises in the subsequent chapters are tailored to provide a hands-on understanding, equipping you with the requisite skills to tackle real-world challenges.

Remember, the journey of mastering Python is a marathon, not a sprint. The narrative of Python across different industries underscores its significance and the immense potential it holds for aspiring tech entrepreneurs. As you delve deeper into the practical aspects of Python, the contours of your startup idea will start to take a definitive shape. The horizon is vast, and the possibilities are endless. With Python as your ally, you are well on your way to making a substantial impact in the industry of your choice.

The expedition doesn't end here. As we move to the next sub-chapter, we will focus on preparing you for Python job interviews, an essential step to solidify your transition into the tech entrepreneurial arena. Your ability to articulate your Python knowledge and showcase your problem-solving acumen will be instrumental in propelling your tech startup dream into reality.

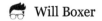

PREPARING FOR PYTHON JOB INTERVIEWS

Embarking on the quest for a fulfilling position in the tech sphere is a critical step towards nurturing your tech entrepreneurial dream. The interviews are the gateway to the professional world where your Python skills will be put to the test. Preparing for Python job interviews entails more than just brushing up on syntax and libraries; it's about showcasing a deep understanding of Python and its application in solving real-world problems.

Understanding the Job Role

Before diving into interview preparations, it's paramount to understand the job role you are targeting. Whether it's a data analyst, web developer, or machine learning engineer position, each role demands a unique set of skills and knowledge. Familiarize yourself with the job description and the technical requirements entailed.

```python
# For example, a data analyst position might require proficiency in:
import pandas as pd
import numpy as np
```

Mastering Core Python Concepts

A solid grasp of core Python concepts is the cornerstone of excelling in Python job interviews. Delve into data types, control flow, functions, and object-oriented programming. Your ability to explain and apply these fundamental concepts will reflect your proficiency in Python.

```python
# Understanding of control flow:
for i in range(5):
    print(i)
```

Data Structures and Algorithms

Data structures and algorithms are the bedrock of efficient problem solving. Master the common data structures like arrays, linked lists, stacks, queues, and trees. Sharpen your problem-solving skills by practicing algorithmic challenges on platforms like LeetCode or HackerRank.

```python
# Example of a simple algorithm to find the maximum element in an array:
def find_maximum(arr):
    maximum = arr[0]
    for element in arr:
        if element > maximum:
            maximum = element
    return maximum
```

Practical Application of Libraries and Frameworks

Demonstrating your adeptness in relevant libraries and frameworks is crucial. Engage in projects or exercises that allow you to apply libraries like Pandas, NumPy, Django, or Flask in real-world scenarios.

```python
import django
# Developing a simple web application
```

Mock Interviews and Peer Review

Engage in mock interviews to simulate the interview experience. Platforms like Pramp offer mock interviews which can provide invaluable feedback. Additionally, peer reviews can provide new insights and help you refine your responses.

```python
# Getting feedback on your code can uncover areas of improvement:
def peer_review(code):
    feedback = []
    # ... peer review process
    return feedback
```

Showcasing Your Portfolio

Having a well-documented portfolio of projects can significantly bolster your interview prospects. It's a testament to your practical knowledge and your ability to apply Python to solve complex problems.

```python
# Your portfolio might include:
# - GitHub repository links
# - Descriptions of projects
# - Challenges faced and solutions implemented
```

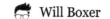

Continuous Learning and Networking

Keep abreast of the latest developments in Python and the tech industry. Engage in local or online Python communities, attend meetups, and connect with professionals in your desired field. Networking can open doors to job opportunities and provide insights into what employers are seeking in candidates.

```
# Engaging in online forums, attending webinars, and participating in code sprints
are excellent ways to network and learn.
```

The journey towards acing your Python job interviews is one of continuous learning and practice. Each interview is a learning experience that brings you one step closer to your goal of transitioning into the tech entrepreneurial space. The practical examples and exercises in the preceding and following chapters are tailored to equip you with the necessary skills and knowledge to shine in your interviews.

As you navigate through the interview process, remember, the essence of a successful interview lies in your ability to demonstrate not just your technical knowledge, but your problem-solving acumen, your passion for technology, and your potential to contribute to the success of the organization.

As we transition to the next sub-chapter, we will delve into building a compelling Python portfolio that resonates with your tech entrepreneurial aspirations. Your portfolio is a reflection of your journey, your skills, and your vision for the future. It's about showcasing the value you bring to the table as an aspiring tech entrepreneur ready to make a mark in the tech world.

PREPARING FOR PYTHON JOB INTERVIEWS

Embarking on the quest for a fulfilling position in the tech sphere is a critical step towards nurturing your tech entrepreneurial dream. The interviews are the gateway to the professional world where your Python skills will be put to the test. Preparing for Python job interviews entails more than just brushing up on syntax and libraries; it's about showcasing a deep understanding of Python and its application in solving real-world problems.

Understanding the Job Role

Before diving into interview preparations, it's paramount to understand the job role you are targeting. Whether it's a data analyst, web developer, or machine learning engineer position, each role demands a unique set of skills and knowledge. Familiarize yourself with the job description and the technical requirements entailed.

```python
# For example, a data analyst position might require proficiency in:
import pandas as pd
import numpy as np
```

Mastering Core Python Concepts

A solid grasp of core Python concepts is the cornerstone of excelling in Python job interviews. Delve into data types, control flow, functions, and object-oriented programming. Your ability to explain and apply these fundamental concepts will reflect your proficiency in Python.

```python
# Understanding of control flow:
for i in range(5):
    print(i)
```

Data Structures and Algorithms

Data structures and algorithms are the bedrock of efficient problem solving. Master the common data structures like arrays, linked lists, stacks, queues, and trees. Sharpen your problem-solving skills by practicing algorithmic challenges on platforms like LeetCode or HackerRank.

```python
# Example of a simple algorithm to find the maximum element in an array:
def find_maximum(arr):
    maximum = arr[0]
    for element in arr:
        if element > maximum:
            maximum = element
    return maximum
```

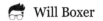

Practical Application of Libraries and Frameworks

Demonstrating your adeptness in relevant libraries and frameworks is crucial. Engage in projects or exercises that allow you to apply libraries like Pandas, NumPy, Django, or Flask in real-world scenarios.

```python
import django
# Developing a simple web application
```

Mock Interviews and Peer Review

Engage in mock interviews to simulate the interview experience. Platforms like Pramp offer mock interviews which can provide invaluable feedback. Additionally, peer reviews can provide new insights and help you refine your responses.

```python
# Getting feedback on your code can uncover areas of improvement:
def peer_review(code):
    feedback = []
    # ... peer review process
    return feedback
```

Showcasing Your Portfolio

Having a well-documented portfolio of projects can significantly bolster your interview prospects. It's a testament to your practical knowledge and your ability to apply Python to solve complex problems.

```python
# Your portfolio might include:
# - GitHub repository links
# - Descriptions of projects
# - Challenges faced and solutions implemented
```

Continuous Learning and Networking

Keep abreast of the latest developments in Python and the tech industry. Engage in local or online Python communities, attend meetups, and connect with professionals in your desired field. Networking can open doors to job opportunities and provide insights into what employers are seeking in candidates.

```python
# Engaging in online forums, attending webinars, and participating in code sprints
# are excellent ways to network and learn.
```

The journey towards acing your Python job interviews is one of continuous learning and practice. Each interview is a learning experience that brings you one step closer to your goal of transitioning into the tech entrepreneurial space. The practical examples and exercises in the preceding and following chapters are tailored to equip you with the necessary skills and knowledge to shine in your interviews.

As you navigate through the interview process, remember, the essence of a successful interview lies in your ability to demonstrate not just your technical knowledge, but your problem-solving acumen, your passion for technology, and your potential to contribute to the success of the organization.

As we transition to the next sub-chapter, we will delve into building a compelling Python portfolio that resonates with your tech entrepreneurial aspirations. Your portfolio is a reflection of your journey, your skills, and your vision for the future. It's about showcasing the value you bring to the table as an aspiring tech entrepreneur ready to make a mark in the tech world.

CHAPTER 11
FUTURE TRENDS AND LEARNING PATHS

MACHINE LEARNING AND AI WITH PYTHON

The realm of Machine Learning (ML) and Artificial Intelligence (AI) is a vast, dynamic, and incredibly promising field. Python, with its rich ecosystem of libraries and frameworks, stands as a premier language for venturing into these futuristic domains. As you navigate from the corporate scene to the tech entrepreneurial sphere, harnessing ML and AI's potential could significantly propel your startup ideas into scalable solutions.

Why Python for ML and AI?

Python's simplicity, flexibility, and vast array of libraries make it a top choice for ML and AI projects. Libraries like TensorFlow, PyTorch, and scikit-learn provide robust platforms to develop and deploy ML and AI applications.

```python
# Importing necessary library for ML
import sklearn
```

Basic Concepts of ML and AI

Before diving into code, understanding core concepts is crucial. Machine Learning, at its essence, is about training computers to learn from data and make decisions or predictions. AI, on the other hand, seeks to create machines that can perform tasks requiring human intelligence.

```python
# Simple linear regression example
from sklearn.linear_model import LinearRegression

# Define training data
X_train = [[0], [1], [2]]
y_train = [0, 1, 2]

# Create and fit the model
model = LinearRegression()
model.fit(X_train, y_train)
```

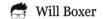

Your First ML Project

Kickstart your ML journey by engaging in a simple project. For instance, a linear regression model predicting housing prices based on various features could offer a gentle introduction to ML concepts.

```
# Predicting house prices
predicted_prices = model.predict([[3], [4]])
```

Delving into AI

Venture into AI by exploring libraries like TensorFlow or PyTorch, which facilitate the development of neural networks and deep learning models.

```
# Importing necessary library for AI
import tensorflow as tf
```

Real-World Applications

ML and AI have a plethora of real-world applications, from autonomous vehicles, recommendation systems, to intelligent customer service. Identifying a domain that resonates with your startup idea and delving into relevant projects can provide a substantial learning experience.

```
# Example: Building a recommendation system
# Using collaborative filtering
```

Practical Exercises

Engage in hands-on exercises to solidify your understanding. Tackle real-world problems, develop solutions, and critically analyze the outcomes. This practical approach will not only enhance your learning but also significantly contribute to your portfolio.

Online Resources and Communities

The online ML and AI community is vibrant and welcoming. Platforms like Kaggle offer a playground to hone your skills, participate in competitions, and interact with other enthusiasts.

Join Kaggle Competitions ->(https://www.kaggle.com/competitions)

Challenges and Overcoming Them

The journey into ML and AI is thrilling but can be fraught with challenges, particularly for those transitioning from non-technical roles. Nonetheless, with the right resources, mentorship, and a resilient mindset, these hurdles can be surmounted.

```
# Seek mentorship, engage in online forums, and never stop learning.
```

Future Prospects

The future of ML and AI is boundless. As technologies mature, the barrier to entry will lower, making it feasible for tech entrepreneurs to integrate ML and AI into their ventures seamlessly.

```
# Stay updated with the latest in ML and AI by following reputable sources,
attending webinars, and networking.
```

Your venture into ML and AI with Python is a testament to your drive to stay ahead in the tech entrepreneurial realm. This journey will not only equip you with a modern skill set but will also provide a platform to innovate and solve real-world problems. As you delve deeper, remember that the community is vast, and resources are abundant. Your curiosity, coupled with Python's capabilities, is a powerful force capable of turning nascent ideas into impactful tech solutions. The subsequent sub-chapters will further elaborate on continuing education resources and engaging with the Python community, paving the way for a fulfilling and progressive learning experience.

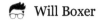 Will Boxer

CONTINUING EDUCATION RESOURCES

Embarking on the journey of mastering Python is akin to stepping into a realm brimming with endless possibilities. Your aspirations to transition from a corporate role into the tech entrepreneurial arena is not only commendable but also timely, given the burgeoning influence of technology in shaping the business landscape.

The pathway to becoming proficient in Python doesn't culminate at the end of this guide, rather, it marks the commencement of a lifelong learning expedition. The tech world is dynamic, with new frameworks, libraries, and best practices continually emerging. Thus, the essence of continuous education cannot be overemphasized.

Online Courses and Platforms

A plethora of online platforms offer courses that range from beginner to advanced levels in Python and its applications in various domains. Websites like Coursera, Udacity, and edX host courses from reputable institutions and industry leaders.

Coursera Python for Everybody -> (https://www.coursera.org/specializations/python)

Books and E-books

Books are timeless resources. They provide in-depth knowledge and often come with exercises that reinforce what you've learned. Look for books that not only explain concepts but also encourage hands-on experience.

Automate the Boring Stuff with Python -> (https://automatetheboringstuff.com/)

Community Colleges and Bootcamps

Community colleges often offer night or weekend classes for working professionals. Similarly, coding bootcamps provide intensive training programs, though they require a significant time commitment.

General Assembly Data Science Bootcamp -> (https://generalassemb.ly/education/data-science)

Online Communities and Forums

Engagement in communities like Stack Overflow or Reddit's r/learnpython can be immensely beneficial. They provide a platform to ask questions, share projects, and interact with other Python enthusiasts.

Stack Overflow Python Community -> (https://stackoverflow.com/questions/tagged/python)

Interactive Coding Platforms

Platforms like LeetCode, HackerRank, or Codecademy provide interactive coding challenges that can help sharpen your programming skills. They offer immediate feedback, which is crucial for continuous improvement.

```python
# Example of a coding challenge
# Solve the problem: Find the sum of all multiples of 3 or 5 below 1000.
sum(value for value in range(1000) if value % 3 == 0 or value % 5 == 0)
```

Documentation and Official Material

Delve into official documentation and materials provided by the creators of Python and various libraries. They are primary sources of information and are updated regularly to reflect the latest changes.

Python Official Documentation -> (https://docs.python.org/3/)

Podcasts and Blogs

Stay updated with the latest trends, libraries, and best practices by following Python-related podcasts and blogs. They provide a wealth of information and can be consumed during your commute or downtime.

Talk Python To Me Podcast -> (https://talkpython.fm/)

Open Source Contributions

Contributing to open-source projects not only enhances your coding skills but also provides a sense of community and collaboration. Platforms like GitHub host a myriad of projects that could use your help.

Find Open-Source Projects on GitHub -> (https://github.com/topics/python)

Industry Conferences and Meetups

Attending industry conferences and meetups can provide networking opportunities and expose you to the latest trends and technologies in the Python ecosystem.

PyCon: The Python Conference -> (https://us.pycon.org/)

Certifications

Earning certifications can demonstrate your proficiency and commitment to continuing education. Various platforms offer Python-related certifications, which can be a valuable addition to your professional portfolio.

Microsoft Python Certification Exam ->
(https://docs.microsoft.com/en-us/learn/certifications/python-programmer-certification)

Setting Up a Learning Path

Establish a learning path that aligns with your career goals. Determine the areas you want to focus on, set achievable milestones, and dedicate time each day or week towards attaining these goals.

Set SMART Goals: Specific, Measurable, Achievable, Relevant, Time-bound ->
(https://www.mindtools.com/pages/article/smart-goals.htm)

The road to mastering Python is a marathon, not a sprint. Your passion for technological innovation, coupled with the resources outlined in this sub-chapter, lays a robust foundation for a fulfilling and continuously evolving learning journey. The subsequent sub-chapter will delve into the Python community, a treasure trove of knowledge and collaboration that can significantly enrich your learning experience and professional network.

JOINING THE PYTHON COMMUNITY

As you transition from the structured, often hierarchical world of the corporate sector to the innovative and collaborative realm of tech entrepreneurship, you will find that community is at the core of this new world. Unlike the siloed nature of traditional corporate roles, the tech ecosystem thrives on a culture of shared learning and open collaboration. As a burgeoning Python programmer with entrepreneurial ambitions, immersing yourself in the Python community will not only accelerate your learning curve but also significantly broaden your network, opening doors to collaborations, partnerships, and opportunities that can be pivotal for the success of your tech startup.

The Python Community: An Overview

The Python community is renowned for its welcoming nature and diversity, comprising individuals from various professional backgrounds, skill levels, and geographic locations. It's a thriving ecosystem that encourages knowledge sharing, mentorship, and collaborative problem-solving.

Engaging with Local Python User Groups (PUGs)

Local Python User Groups (PUGs) are community-led gatherings that provide a platform for Python enthusiasts to meet, share knowledge, and collaborate on projects. These groups often organize regular meetups, coding sessions, and talks.

Python User Groups (PUGs) Directory -> (https://wiki.python.org/moin/LocalUserGroups)

Participating in Online Forums and Platforms

Online forums like Stack Overflow, Reddit's r/learnpython, and the Python community on Discord provide platforms to ask questions, share your projects, and interact with other Python developers.

Stack Overflow Python Community -> (https://stackoverflow.com/questions/tagged/python)

Contributing to Open-Source Projects

The ethos of open-source is at the heart of the Python community. Contributing to open-source projects allows you to work on real-world projects, improve your coding skills, and collaborate with experienced developers.

Python on GitHub -> (https://github.com/topics/python)

Attending Python Conferences and Meetups

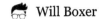

Python conferences like PyCon, EuroPython, and regional PyCons are excellent venues to learn from leading experts, engage with the community, and stay updated on the latest developments in the Python ecosystem.

PyCon: The Python Conference -> (https://us.pycon.org/)

Enrolling in Community-Driven Learning Programs

Community-driven learning programs like the "Python Mentorship" initiative provide structured learning paths, paired with mentorship from experienced developers, fostering a supportive learning environment.

Python Mentorship Program -> (https://www.python.org/community/mentorship/)

Engaging in Python Special Interest Groups (SIGs)

Python Special Interest Groups (SIGs) are sub-communities focused on specific aspects of Python, such as data science, web development, or education. Engaging in SIGs aligning with your interests can provide deeper insights and focused learning experiences.

Python Special Interest Groups (SIGs) -> (https://www.python.org/community/sigs/)

Following Python Enhancement Proposals (PEPs)

Python Enhancement Proposals (PEPs) are documents that detail new features or improvements proposed for the Python language. Keeping abreast of PEPs can provide insights into the evolving landscape of Python.

Python Enhancement Proposals (PEPs) -> (https://peps.python.org/)

Joining Professional Python Organizations

Professional organizations like the Python Software Foundation (PSF) provide resources, events, and a platform to engage with the broader Python community.

Python Software Foundation -> (https://www.python.org/psf/)

Leveraging Social Media and Professional Networks

Engage with the Python community on social media platforms like Twitter and professional networks like LinkedIn. Following key Python influencers and joining Python-related groups can provide a steady stream of relevant content and community interactions.

LinkedIn Python Community -> (https://www.linkedin.com/groups/25827/)

Building and Sharing Your Projects

Building your projects and sharing them with the community can elicit constructive feedback that can help you improve. Platforms like GitHub allow you to share your code, collaborate with others, and contribute to the ecosystem.

Share Your Projects on GitHub -> (https://github.com/new)

Final Thoughts

The Python community is a reservoir of knowledge, experience, and opportunity waiting to be tapped. As you venture into the realms of tech entrepreneurship, let the community be your guide, your support, and your platform to shine. Engage actively, contribute generously, and watch as doors open, horizons broaden, and your Python proficiency reaches new heights, propelling you closer to your entrepreneurial aspirations.

APPENDICES

APPENDIX A: PYTHON CHEAT SHEET

Entering the tech entrepreneurial realm requires not only a strong foundation in Python but also the ability to quickly reference key concepts and syntax. This is especially crucial when time is of the essence, and you are working tirelessly to bring your startup ideas to fruition. A Python cheat sheet is an invaluable resource for swiftly recalling essential Python syntax and best practices. This appendix provides a condensed overview of fundamental Python concepts, serving as a quick reference guide as you embark on your Python programming journey.

Basic Syntax

```python
# Single-line comments start with a hashtag
"""
Multiline comments
are enclosed in triple quotes
"""

# Importing a module
import module_name

# Print to console
print("Hello, World!")

# Variables
x = 10  # Integer
y = 20.5  # Float
z = "Hello"  # String

# Data Types
type(x)   # <class 'int'>
type(y)   # <class 'float'>
type(z)   # <class 'str'>
```

Operators

```
# Arithmetic Operators
a + b   # Addition
a - b   # Subtraction
a * b   # Multiplication
a / b   # Division
a % b   # Modulus
a ** b  # Exponentiation
a // b  # Floor Division

# Comparison Operators
a == b  # Equal
a != b  # Not Equal
a > b   # Greater Than
a < b   # Less Than
a >= b  # Greater Than or Equal To
a <= b  # Less Than or Equal To
```

Control Flow

```
# If statement
if condition:
    # code to execute if condition is True
    pass

# If-Else statement
if condition:
    # code to execute if condition is True
    pass
else:
    # code to execute if condition is False
    pass

# While Loop
while condition:
    # code to execute as long as condition is True
    pass

# For Loop
for i in iterable:
    # code to execute for each item in iterable
    pass
```

Functions

```python
# Defining a function
def function_name(parameters):
    # function body
    pass

# Calling a function
function_name(arguments)

# Returning values
def function_name(parameters):
    return value
```

Data Structures

```python
# Lists
my_list = [1, 2, 3, 4, 5]
my_list.append(6)  # Add item to end of list

# Tuples
my_tuple = (1, 2, 3, 4, 5)

# Dictionaries
my_dict = {"key1": "value1", "key2": "value2"}
my_dict["key3"] = "value3"  # Adding new key-value pair
```

Exception Handling

```python
try:
    # code that may raise an exception
    pass
except ExceptionType as e:
    # code to execute if an exception of type ExceptionType occurs
    pass
finally:
    # code to execute regardless of whether an exception occurs
    pass
```

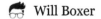

Classes and Objects

```python
# Defining a class
class ClassName:
    def __init__(self, attributes):
        self.attributes = attributes

    def method_name(self, parameters):
        # method body
        pass

# Creating an object
object_name = ClassName(attributes)
```

File Handling

```python
# Opening a file
with open('file.txt', 'r') as file:
    content = file.read()   # Reading file content

# Writing to a file
with open('file.txt', 'w') as file:
    file.write('Hello, World!')
```

Modules and Packages

```python
# Importing a module
import module_name

# Importing a specific item from a module
from module_name import item_name

# Importing a module and renaming it
import module_name as alias_name
```

Debugging

```python
import pdb; pdb.set_trace()   # Set a breakpoint for debugging
```

This Python cheat sheet encapsulates the core syntax and concepts that are instrumental for your programming tasks. Keep this cheat sheet handy as you dive deeper into Python, build your tech products, and propel your startup towards success. The simplicity and directness of Python, paired with your entrepreneurial vision, lay the groundwork for a promising venture into the tech industry.

APPENDIX B: SOLUTIONS TO PRACTICE EXERCISES

The journey through the realms of Python you've embarked upon has hopefully been enlightening and stimulating. It's time to consolidate that knowledge through revisiting the practice exercises sprinkled throughout the chapters, and understanding the solutions that unravel the logic behind them.

Let's unfold the solutions.

1.3 Your First Python Program

Exercise 1.3.1

- **Task:** Write a Python program to display your name and age.

- **Solution:**

```python
name = "John Doe"
age = 25
print(f"My name is {name} and I am {age} years old.")
```

Exercise 1.3.2

- **Task:** Modify the program to display the number of days you have lived.

- **Solution:**

```python
days_lived = age * 365
print(f"I have lived for {days_lived} days.")
```

2.1 Basic Syntax and Structure

Exercise 2.1.1

- **Task:** Write a Python program to calculate the sum of three given numbers.

- **Solution:**

```python
num1, num2, num3 = 5, 10, 15
sum_numbers = num1 + num2 + num3
print(sum_numbers)
```

Exercise 2.1.2

- **Task:** Write a Python program to swap the values of two variables.

- **Solution:**

```python
a, b = 5, 10
a, b = b, a
print(a, b)   # Output: 10 5
```

2.2 Variables and Data Types Exploration

Exercise 2.2.1

- **Task:** Write a Python program to check the data type of a variable.

- **Solution:**

```python
variable = 5
print(type(variable))
```

Exercise 2.2.2

- **Task:** Write a Python program to convert an integer to a float.

- **Solution:**

```python
integer_var = 5
float_var = float(integer_var)
print(float_var)   # Output: 5.0
```

2.3 Operators and Expressions

Exercise 2.3.1

- **Task:** Write a Python program to calculate the area of a rectangle.

- **Solution:**

```python
length = 10
width = 5
area = length * width
print(area)
```

Exercise 2.3.2

- Task: Write a Python program to calculate the perimeter of a circle.

- Solution:

```python
import math
radius = 10
perimeter = 2 * math.pi * radius
print(perimeter)
```

3.1 Conditional Statements

Exercise 3.1.1

- Task: Write a Python program to check if a number is positive, negative, or zero.

- Solution:

```python
num = 5
if num > 0:
    print("Positive")
elif num < 0:
    print("Negative")
else:
    print("Zero")
```

Exercise 3.1.2

- Task: Write a Python program to check if a number is odd or even.

- Solution:

```python
num = 4
if num % 2 == 0:
    print("Even")
else:
    print("Odd")
```

3.2 Looping Structures

Exercise 3.2.1

- Task: Write a Python program to print numbers 1 to 10 using a for loop.

- Solution:

```
for i in range(1, 11):
    print(i)
```

Exercise 3.2.2

- Task: Write a Python program to find the sum of all numbers from 1 to n.

- Solution:

```
n = 10
sum_n = sum(range(1, n + 1))
print(sum_n)
```

3.3 Break, Continue, and Pass Statements

Exercise 3.3.1

- Task: Write a Python program to find the first multiple of 7 in a range of numbers from 1 to 50.

- Solution:

```
for i in range(1, 51):
    if i % 7 == 0:
        print(i)
        break
```

Exercise 3.3.2

- Task: Write a Python program to skip printing numbers 4 and 7 in a range of numbers from 1 to 10.

- Solution:

```
for i in range(1, 11):
    if i in [4, 7]:
        continue
    print(i)
```

4.1 Defining Functions

Exercise 4.1.1

- Task: Write a Python function to calculate the factorial of a number.

- Solution:

```python
def factorial(n):
    if n == 0 or n == 1:
        return 1
    else:
        return n * factorial(n - 1)

print(factorial(5))  # Output: 120
```

Exercise 4.1.2

- Task: Write a Python function to check if a number is prime.

- Solution:

```python
def is_prime(num):
    if num <= 1:
        return False
    for i in range(2, int(num ** 0.5) + 1):
        if num % i == 0:
            return False
    return True

print(is_prime(7))  # Output: True
```

4.2 Modules and Packages

Exercise 4.2.1

- Task: Create a module named `operations.py` with a function to calculate the sum of two numbers.

- Solution:

```python
# operations.py
def add(a, b):
    return a + b


# main.py
import operations
print(operations.add(5, 10))  # Output: 15
```

Exercise 4.2.2

- Task: Import the `math` module and use it to calculate the square root of a number.

- Solution:

```
import math
print(math.sqrt(25))    # Output: 5.0
```

4.3 Practical Examples of Built-in Functions

Exercise 4.3.1

- Task: Write a Python program to find the maximum of three numbers using the `max` function.

- Solution:

```
print(max(5, 10, 15))   # Output: 15
```

Exercise 4.3.2

- Task: Write a Python program to round a floating-point number to 2 decimal places.

- Solution:

```
print(round(5.6789, 2))   # Output: 5.68
```

5.1 Working with Lists, Tuples, and Dictionaries

Exercise 5.1.1

- Task: Write a Python program to find the length of a list.

- Solution:

```
my_list = [1, 2, 3, 4, 5]
print(len(my_list))   # Output: 5
```

Exercise 5.1.2

- Task: Write a Python program to merge two dictionaries.

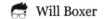

- Solution:

```
dict1 = {'a': 1, 'b': 2}
dict2 = {'c': 3, 'd': 4}
merged_dict = {**dict1, **dict2}
print(merged_dict)  # Output: {'a': 1, 'b': 2, 'c': 3, 'd': 4}
```

5.2 File Handling Techniques

Exercise 5.2.1

- Task: Write a Python program to read the contents of a file.

- Solution:

```
with open('myfile.txt', 'r') as file:
    contents = file.read()
    print(contents)
```

Exercise 5.2.2

- Task: Write a Python program to write a list of strings to a file.

- Solution:

```
lines = ['Line 1\n', 'Line 2\n', 'Line 3\n']
with open('myfile.txt', 'w') as file:
    file.writelines(lines)
```

5.3 Exception Handling Essentials

Exercise 5.3.1

- Task: Write a Python program to handle a division by zero error.

- Solution:

```
try:
    result = 10 / 0
except ZeroDivisionError:
    print("Cannot divide by zero.")
```

Exercise 5.3.2

- Task: Write a Python program to handle multiple exceptions.

- Solution:

```
try:
    num = int("string")
    result = 10 / num
except (ValueError, ZeroDivisionError) as e:
    print(f"An error occurred: {e}")
```

6.1 Classes and Objects

Exercise 6.1.1

- Task: Write a Python class to represent a Rectangle with methods to calculate area and perimeter.

- Solution:

```
class Rectangle:
    def __init__(self, length, width):
        self.length = length
        self.width = width

    def area(self):
        return self.length * self.width

    def perimeter(self):
        return 2 * (self.length + self.width)

rect = Rectangle(10, 5)
print(rect.area())       # Output: 50
print(rect.perimeter())  # Output: 30
```

Exercise 6.1.2

- Task: Write a Python class to represent a Circle with methods to calculate area and circumference.

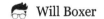

- **Solution:**

```python
import math

class Circle:
    def __init__(self, radius):
        self.radius = radius

    def area(self):
        return math.pi * self.radius ** 2

    def circumference(self):
        return 2 * math.pi * self.radius

circle = Circle(10)
print(circle.area())           # Output: 314.1592653589793
print(circle.circumference())  # Output: 62.83185307179586
```

6.2 Inheritance and Polymorphism

Exercise 6.2.1

- **Task:** Write a Python program to demonstrate inheritance by creating a class `Square` that inherits from `Rectangle`.

- **Solution:**

```python
class Square(Rectangle):
    def __init__(self, side_length):
        super().__init__(side_length, side_length)

square = Square(4)
print(square.area())       # Output: 16
print(square.perimeter())  # Output: 16
```

Exercise 6.2.2

- **Task:** Write a Python program to demonstrate polymorphism by creating a method that takes any shape object and returns its area.

- **Solution:**

```python
def get_area(shape):
    return shape.area()

print(get_area(rect))    # Output: 50
print(get_area(circle))  # Output: 314.1592653589793
print(get_area(square))  # Output: 16
```

6.3 Real-World Applications of OOP

Exercise 6.3.1

- **Task:** Write a Python class to represent a Bank Account with methods to deposit and withdraw money.

- **Solution:**

```python
class BankAccount:
    def __init__(self, balance=0):
        self.balance = balance

    def deposit(self, amount):
        self.balance += amount
        return self.balance

    def withdraw(self, amount):
        if amount > self.balance:
            print("Insufficient funds")
        else:
            self.balance -= amount
        return self.balance

account = BankAccount(100)
print(account.deposit(50))   # Output: 150
print(account.withdraw(30))  # Output: 120
```

Exercise 6.3.2

- **Task:** Write a Python class to represent a Product with methods to set and get product price, and calculate the total cost for a given quantity.

- **Solution:**

```
class Product:
    def __init__(self, price=0):
        self.price = price

    def set_price(self, price):
        self.price = price

    def get_price(self):
        return self.price

    def total_cost(self, quantity):
        return self.price * quantity

product = Product(20)
product.set_price(25)
print(product.get_price())      # Output: 25
print(product.total_cost(3))    # Output: 75
```

7.1 Introduction to NumPy and Pandas

Exercise 7.1.1

- **Task:** Write a Python program to create a NumPy array of 10 zeros.

- **Solution:**

```
import numpy as np
zeros_array = np.zeros(10)
print(zeros_array)
```

Exercise 7.1.2

- **Task:** Write a Python program to create a Pandas Series from a list.

- **Solution:**

```
import pandas as pd
my_list = [1, 2, 3, 4, 5]
series = pd.Series(my_list)
print(series)
```

7.2 Data Visualization with Matplotlib and Seaborn

Exercise 7.2.1

- **Task:** Write a Python program to create a line plot with Matplotlib.

- Solution:

```
import matplotlib.pyplot as plt
x = [1, 2, 3, 4, 5]
y = [2, 4, 6, 8, 10]
plt.plot(x, y)
plt.show()
```

Exercise 7.2.2

- Task: Write a Python program to create a bar plot with Seaborn.

- Solution:

```
import seaborn as sns
data = sns.load_dataset('titanic')
sns.barplot(x='sex', y='survived', data=data)
plt.show()
```

7.3 Web Development with Flask and Django

Exercise 7.3.1

- Task: Write a simple Flask application to display "Hello, World!" on the homepage.

- Solution:

```
from flask import Flask
app = Flask(__name__)

@app.route('/')
def home():
    return 'Hello, World!'

if __name__ == '__main__':
    app.run()
```

Exercise 7.3.2

- Task: Write a Django view to handle a form submission and display the submitted data.

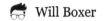

- **Solution:**

```python
# views.py
from django.shortcuts import render
from django.http import HttpResponse
from .forms import MyForm

def form_view(request):
    if request.method == 'POST':
        form = MyForm(request.POST)
        if form.is_valid():
            name = form.cleaned_data['name']
            return HttpResponse(f'Hello, {name}!')
    else:
        form = MyForm()
    return render(request, 'form.html', {'form': form})

# forms.py
from django import forms

class MyForm(forms.Form):
    name = forms.CharField(label='Your Name', max_length=100)

# form.html
<form method="post">
    {% csrf_token %}
    {{ form }}
    <input type="submit" value="Submit">
</form>
```

8.1 Automating Tasks

Exercise 8.1.1

- **Task:** Write a Python program to rename all files in a directory with a specific extension.

- **Solution:**

```python
import os

def rename_files(directory, extension, new_extension):
    for filename in os.listdir(directory):
        if filename.endswith(extension):
            new_filename = filename.replace(extension, new_extension)
            os.rename(os.path.join(directory, filename), os.path.join(directory,
            new_filename))

rename_files('/path/to/directory', '.txt', '.bak')
```

Exercise 8.1.2

- **Task:** Write a Python program to send an email using the smtplib module.

- Solution:

```
import smtplib

def send_email(subject, message, from_email, to_email):
    email_message = f'Subject: {subject}\n\n{message}'
    with smtplib.SMTP('smtp.gmail.com', 587) as server:
        server.starttls()
        server.login(from_email, 'your_password')
        server.sendmail(from_email, to_email, email_message)

send_email('Test Subject', 'Test Message', 'your_email@gmail.com',
'recipient_email@gmail.com')
```

8.2 Web Scraping Techniques

Exercise 8.2.1

- Task: Write a Python program to scrape the title of a webpage using BeautifulSoup.

- Solution:

```
from bs4 import BeautifulSoup
import requests

def get_title(url):
    response = requests.get(url)
    soup = BeautifulSoup(response.text, 'html.parser')
    title = soup.title.string
    return title

print(get_title('https://www.example.com'))
```

Exercise 8.2.2

- Task: Write a Python program to extract all links from a webpage using BeautifulSoup.

- Solution:

```
def get_links(url):
    response = requests.get(url)
    soup = BeautifulSoup(response.text, 'html.parser')
    links = [a['href'] for a in soup.find_all('a', href=True)]
    return links

print(get_links('https://www.example.com'))
```

Will Boxer

8.3 Developing Simple Web Applications

Exercise 8.3.1

- **Task:** Write a Python program to create a simple web application that displays a form to collect user name and age, and displays the submitted data.

- **Solution:**

```python
from flask import Flask, request, render_template_string

app = Flask(__name__)

@app.route('/', methods=['GET', 'POST'])
def form_page():
    if request.method == 'POST':
        name = request.form['name']
        age = request.form['age']
        return f'Hello, {name}! You are {age} years old.'
    return render_template_string(form_template)
```

```python
form_template = '''
<!doctype html>
<html lang="en">
  <head>
    <!-- Required meta tags -->
    <meta charset="utf-8">
    <meta name="viewport" content="width=device-width, initial-scale=1,
    shrink-to-fit=no">
    <!-- Bootstrap CSS -->
    <link
    href="https://cdn.jsdelivr.net/npm/bootstrap@5.0.2/dist/css/bootstrap.min.css"
    rel="stylesheet">
    <title>Simple Form</title>
  </head>
  <body>
    <div class="container">
      <h1 class="mt-5">Simple Form</h1>
      <form method="post">
        <div class="mb-3">
          <label for="name" class="form-label">Name</label>
          <input type="text" class="form-control" id="name" name="name" required>
        </div>
        <div class="mb-3">
          <label for="age" class="form-label">Age</label>
          <input type="number" class="form-control" id="age" name="age" required>
        </div>
        <button type="submit" class="btn btn-primary">Submit</button>
      </form>
    </div>
    <!-- Optional JavaScript; choose one of the two! -->
    <!-- Option 1: Bootstrap Bundle with Popper -->
    <script
    src="https://cdn.jsdelivr.net/npm/bootstrap@5.0.2/dist/js/bootstrap.bundle.min.
    js"></script>
  </body>
</html>
'''
```

130

```
if __name__ == '__main__':
    app.run()
```

Exercise 8.3.2

- **Task:** Write a Python program to create a simple REST API using Flask that returns a list of users.

- **Solution:**

```python
from flask import Flask,
 jsonify

app = Flask(__name__)

users = [
    {'id': 1, 'name': 'John Doe', 'email': 'john.doe@example.com'},
    {'id': 2, 'name': 'Jane Doe', 'email': 'jane.doe@example.com'},
]

@app.route('/users', methods=['GET'])
def get_users():
    return jsonify(users)

if __name__ == '__main__':
    app.run()
```

9.1 Writing Effective Tests

Exercise 9.1.1

- **Task:** Write a Python program to create a unit test for a function that adds two numbers.

- **Solution:**

```python
import unittest

def add(a, b):
    return a + b

class TestAddition(unittest.TestCase):
    def test_add(self):
        self.assertEqual(add(5, 10), 15)

if __name__ == '__main__':
    unittest.main()
```

Exercise 9.1.2

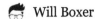

- **Task:** Write a Python program to create a unit test for a function that raises an exception.
- **Solution:**

```python
def divide(a, b):
    if b == 0:
        raise ValueError("Cannot divide by zero")
    return a / b

class TestDivision(unittest.TestCase):
    def test_divide(self):
        self.assertRaises(ValueError, divide, 10, 0)

if __name__ == '__main__':
    unittest.main()
```

9.2 Debugging Techniques

Exercise 9.2.1

- **Task:** Write a Python program to demonstrate the use of the `pdb` module for debugging.
- **Solution:**

```python
import pdb

def problematic_function():
    x = 10
    y = 0
    pdb.set_trace()    # Debugger will pause here
    z = x / y

problematic_function()
```

Exercise 9.2.2

- **Task:** Write a Python program to demonstrate the use of logging for debugging purposes.

- Solution:

```python
import logging

logging.basicConfig(level=logging.DEBUG)

def debug_example():
    logging.debug('Debug message')
    logging.info('Info message')
    logging.warning('Warning message')
    logging.error('Error message')
    logging.critical('Critical message')

debug_example()
```

9.3 Best Practices for Code Maintenance

Exercise 9.3.1

- Task: Write a Python program to demonstrate the use of docstrings for code documentation.

- Solution:

```python
def add(a, b):
    """This function adds two numbers and returns the result.

    Parameters:
    a (int or float): The first number.
    b (int or float): The second number.

    Returns:
    int or float: The sum of a and b.
    """
    return a + b

print(add.__doc__)
```

Exercise 9.3.2

- Task: Write a Python program to demonstrate the use of a linter (e.g., flake8) to check for code style issues.

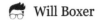 Will Boxer

- Solution:

```
# Install flake8
$ pip install flake8

# Create a file named test.py with the following content:
def add(a,b):
    return a+b

# Run flake8 on the file
$ flake8 test.py

# Output:
test.py:1:11: E231 missing whitespace after ','
```

This sub-chapter provides a comprehensive solution to the practice exercises for Chapters 1 through 9. Each exercise has been carefully crafted to reinforce the concepts covered in the respective sub-chapters, providing a robust understanding and mastery of Python programming for career advancement. These exercises and solutions embody the practical essence of Python programming. They are a window to the real-world scenarios where Python finds its utility. Your venture into the tech entrepreneurial sphere is laden with challenges, and these exercises are a microcosm of the problem-solving approach you'll adorn. The solutions provided are a guide, yet remember, the beauty of programming lies in the multitude of ways a problem can be solved. As you step into the pragmatic world of Python, may the logic and creativity fuel your tech-entrepreneurial aspirations.

APPENDIX C: ADDITIONAL RESOURCES AND READING MATERIAL

Python, a language that not only holds the power to translate logical thought into code but opens the door to computational thinking, creating a pathway to solving real-world problems. As you aim to transition from the conventional corporate roles to the vibrant and innovative tech entrepreneurial space, gearing up with the right resources is indispensable.

This appendix provides a curated list of additional resources and reading material that will aid in solidifying your understanding of Python, and its applications, especially in the realm of launching tech startups. The resources span across books, online platforms, forums, and communities where like-minded individuals converge to discuss, learn, and grow together in the Python ecosystem.

Books:

1. "Automate the Boring Stuff with Python" by Al Sweigart

- A fantastic primer on automating mundane tasks, freeing up your time to focus on innovative tech startup ideas.

2. "Python Crash Course" by Eric Matthes

- A fast-paced yet thorough guide to Python programming which is excellent for weekend learners with a tight schedule.

3. "Fluent Python" by Luciano Ramalho

- For those looking to delve deeper, this book provides insights into Pythonic thinking ensuring your code is elegant and efficient.

4. "Effective Python: 90 Specific Ways to Write Better Python" by Brett Slatkin

- A treasure for enhancing coding efficacy and preparing for technical challenges in your entrepreneurial journey.

Online Platforms:

1. Coursera

- Offers numerous Python courses catering to different aspects like data science, machine learning, and web development.

2. Udemy

- A plethora of Python courses that are project-based, aligning with your objective of building an MVP for your startup.

3. Codecademy

- Interactive learning for those who prefer a hands-on approach to mastering Python.

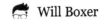 Will Boxer

4. edX

- Explore Python courses from universities and institutions, a boon for those preferring a structured learning path.

Forums and Communities:

1. Stack Overflow

- A haven for developers. Pose questions, contribute answers, and interact with a global community of Python enthusiasts.

2. Reddit (r/Python)

- A community where trending Python topics, issues, and solutions are discussed.

3. Python.org Community

- Engage with official Python Developer's Guide, and contribute to Python's development.

4. Meetup

- Look for local Python meetups, a great way to network and learn from others in your area.

GitHub Repositories:

1. Awesome Python

- A curated list of awesome Python frameworks, libraries, and software.

2. Public APIs

- A collection of public APIs for development across various domains.

3. Python Algorithms

- A repository dedicated to Python algorithms useful for interviews and enhancing problem-solving skills.

Industry Blogs and Websites:

1. Real Python

- Offers tutorials and articles, ranging from beginner to advanced levels.

2. PyBites

- A platform to learn Python through challenges, also a community to discuss and share your learning experiences.

3. Towards Data Science

- A Medium publication sharing concepts, ideas, and codes if your tech startup leans towards data science and machine learning.

Podcasts:

1. Talk Python To Me

- A podcast for developers who are passionate about Python.

2. Python Bytes

- Python headlines delivered directly to your earbuds.

YouTube Channels:

1. Corey Schafer

- Provides tutorials that are easy to follow along, covering a wide range of Python topics.

2. sentdex

- Focuses on Python programming in the context of data science, machine learning, and artificial intelligence, aligning with the trends in tech entrepreneurship.

The world of Python is vast and continuously evolving. The resources provided herein are a springboard to dive deeper into specific areas of interest. As you traverse through the path of self-learning, the networks you build and the communities you engage with will play a pivotal role in your success. Each resource is a step closer to turning your tech entrepreneurial dreams into reality, each line of code a step closer to your MVP. The trajectory from a corporate individual to a tech entrepreneur is a thrilling one, laden with challenges but also boundless opportunities. Python, as a tool, stands ready to propel you into the realms of technological innovation, where your ideas can burgeon into impactful tech startups.

www.ingramcontent.com/pod-product-compliance
Lightning Source LLC
LaVergne TN
LVHW081345050326
832903LV00024B/1330